The Heart of Business

by

Matt Hayes and Jeff Stevens

authorHOUSE™

1663 LIBERTY DRIVE, SUITE 200
BLOOMINGTON, INDIANA 47403
(800) 839-8640
WWW.AUTHORHOUSE.COM

First published by AuthorHouse 11/11/05

ISBN: 1-4208-9663-6 (sc)

Library of Congress Control Number: 2005909688

Printed in the United States of America
Bloomington, Indiana

This book is printed on acid-free paper.

Acknowledgements

Deciding to write a book, especially for two relative novices like ourselves, is a leap. Without the encouragement and extraordinary support of so many people, this book would have remained nothing more than an intriguing daydream and some unfinished thoughts on a whiteboard. We are grateful to God for the friends, counselors, and companies that have encouraged us, read chapters for us, wrestled over scripture with us, and shared generously from their time, hearts, pocketbooks, and life stories.

Thanks to Jon Walters for his wholehearted interest in this project, his steadfast belief in the supremacy of the scriptures, and his generous support that saw this book through its last stages. Without his generous support, this book would remain ¾ finished. We are always thanking God for Pastor John Sale, who has been a faithful minister of the Gospel, pointing us ever and always back to Jesus Christ and His beauty. Thanks to Bruce Barbour of Literary Management Group for his interest in this project, and his ongoing encouragement, reading, and edits.

Brian Buffini has been a wonderful supporter of this project and helped us to believe that we should write a book. We benefited greatly from the opportunity to work closely with his company and to see first hand the power of a point.

Thanks also to Jon, Pastor Sale, Bruce, and Brian as well as Zach Hayes, Paul Swanson, Jim Dismore, Bill French, Mike Peterson, James Lawrence, and Jay Latimer for their critical thoughts and kind but ever honest edits and feedback.

Thanks be to our God and all honor to His Son Jesus Christ for His life. May He glorify Himself through this small book.

Dedication

To Bretta - you are a daily reminder of God's grace in my life, my true friend and lover.

-M.H.

To Jill – You are a true living testimony of what this book is about. You manage our household with the heart of Jesus. With a special thanks to my children, Karlie, Mikayla, Alexandra and Emma Grace.

-J.S.

Table of Contents

If you are looking for another business book that helps you rethink your profit motive and set new management techniques into play that will aid and assist in meeting your goals, put this book back on the shelf and keep looking for the silver bullet.

But if you are serious about learning the questions that will challenge you and your colleagues to consider a completely new paradigm for your business, one grounded in the value of people over profit and motivation over mission, then don't walk out of the store without this book!

Matt Hayes and Jeff Stevens are onto something that will change the way business is done. It's so simple yet so profound: businesses today must change from being profit-motivated to people-motivated so management, owners, employees and customers can share in a higher purpose together. Each will be fulfilled in their contribution to the process; for those working for the company, a sense of belonging to a community committed to their personal improvement and growth and, for the customer, receiving higher value for the dollar invested.

The Heart of Business will not be like any other business book you've read. Matt and Jeff will ask you more questions than they will answer but in the process, I am confident you will get answers to the challenges you have with high turnover, low productivity, lack of motivation and creativity, employee theft and customer complaints. "What's the point in maximizing profit if we minimize our people?" they will ask and then show you why and how to adjust your thinking and systems so you can provide lasting benefits to your people. Drawing examples from companies of excellence they have worked with over the years, as well as their own personal experience as successful entrepreneurs and managers, Matt and Jeff will give you the tools you need to realize the dreams you have for your work and your fellow workers.

Bruce R. Barbour
Founder and President, Literary Management Group, Inc.

Known to friends and colleagues as "BRB," Bruce is in the fourth generation of a family that has served Christian authors and publishers for over one hundred thirty years. In 1870, his great-grand uncle, Fleming H. Revell started publishing Christian books with his brother-in-law, Dwight L. Moody. Following in the footsteps of his grandfather, father and uncle, Bruce joined the Fleming H. Revell Company after graduating with Honors from Pepperdine University in 1975. His publishing career includes: Positions at the Fleming H. Revell Company: Acquisition Editor, Sales Manager and Vice President of Sales and Marketing. Co-founder of Barbour and Company, a promotional book publishing house specializing in Christian books at bargain prices. He served as Executive Vice-President supervising sales, marketing, product development and operations. Joined Thomas Nelson as Vice President, Marketing and served as Vice President, Publisher until leaving in July, 1993 for a six-month sabbatical. In May, Bruce founded Moorings, a Christian Book Division of Random House Publishers and served as Vice President, Publisher. Currently Bruce is the Founder and President of Literary Management Group, Inc., an intellectual property development company that serves authors, writers and companies in the development and distribution of Christian and Inspirational content.

Foreword – James Dismore

When I received a call from Jeff and Matt requesting that I read the transcript of their newly completed book, I was delighted to do so. I knew before I even read it that the book would be an excellent one. My expectations were not disappointed -- my sense was right.

Wow! Every leader, business and otherwise who desires to enhance their life should read this book. It contains so many valuable techniques, strategies and life-changing information. It not only contains excellent techniques and practices for your business, but effective practices for your professional, personal and spiritual life as well. If all of us would only practice and implement what is contained in the pages of this book, OUR LIVES AND OUR COMPANIES WOULD NEVER BE THE SAME AGAIN!

Like many of you, I have read many books. This one is very special. I highly recommend it to everyone. However, hold on because you are in for a life-changing experience.

Jim Dismore
Chairman / CEO Ultimate Support Systems, Fort Collins, Colorado

Founder and Chairman of Kingdom Way Companies, Fort Collins, Colorado

Jim Dismore has more than four decades of experience in retailing and manufacturing. He spent twelve years at Wal-Mart as one of the original officers working directly with Sam Walton, and was Senior Vice President when he left the company. After a series of CEO and senior management positions with major retail chains and manufacturing companies, Jim became President and CEO of Ultimate Support Systems in 1989. In 1994 he became chairman and majority stock holder.

Jim has been mentoring and advising company and spiritual leaders for over 20 years, out of his desire to advance the kingdom of God in the workplace. He has served on the director and advisory boards of Fortune 500 companies and over 30 other companies ranging in size from small start-ups to those with over 500,000 employees. Jim is currently serving on the International Board of Directors for Crown/FCCI ministries. His quest to impact the business community led Jim and his wife, Margaret, to form Kingdom Way Companies.

> *"If you have any encouragement from being united with
> Christ, if any comfort from his love, if any fellowship with the
> Spirit, if any tenderness and compassion, then make my joy
> complete by being like-minded, having the same love, **being
> one in spirit and purpose.**" - Philippians 2:1-2*

The intersection and success of American capitalism and communication technology has produced what is arguably the most abundant society in the history of humankind. Much of what Americans have come to expect as basic necessity is indeed considered extravagant luxury by the majority of the world's other citizens. It is this unprecedented abundance and opportunity which has provided tremendous credibility to a new cultural age.

This 'new age' is commonly referred to as the 'information age', 'technology age', or alternately the 'information technology age'. While information technology has *given rise to this new age,* it is likely not the age itself. The free and open access to information created by technology systems such as the Internet, as well as the tremendous increase in worker productivity which has resulted from electronic connectivity and personal computing platforms have provided the catalyst, context, and even platform for this age, but they are not the age themselves. How history will ultimately define and coin this age is in fact yet to be determined. What is certain is that it is an age of tremendous opportunity and change.

In this age, companies have a greater influence on our lives than do our national government or any other civil authority. As a general rule, the decisions made in the Board Rooms of today's companies have a significantly greater impact on an individual employee's day-to-day material, relational, and spiritual life than do the entirety of the bills and resolutions passed by the U.S. Congress in a single year. Both large and small, today's companies and corporations are the kingdoms of modern day.

Modern companies have become stages upon which the full spectrum of human experience may be expressed and discovered. Provision, validation, toil, blessing, disappointment, loyalty, betrayal, greed, friendship, and love can all be experienced within the context of the modern company.

Although companies remain distinctly human organizations, the size, complexity, and technological systemization of businesses often depersonalize them. To employees and customers alike, companies can become faceless organizations and simple mechanisms to achieve a desired end. It is easy to forget that businesses don't run themselves, and businesses don't run other businesses. People do.

People dream them up, plan them, invest in them, build them, impart vision to them and lead them. In fact, most businesses are organized as a 'company'; a word whose primary definition is simply, "A group of persons."

These 'companies' of men and women are the most powerful and pervasive organizing force within our society. Nearly all of modern life; our families, friends, home, work, food, and fun are somehow either provided for, bought, sold, delivered, created, or discarded by companies.

More than mere agents of provision and wealth generation, modern companies are indeed the many stages upon which the Lord is currently producing much of today's great human drama.

Every cultural age is clothed in a distinct fabric of values and ideals that are championed, encouraged, and rewarded by that particular culture. The Age of Enlightenment esteemed and rewarded intellect, reason, and logic above all else. The Renaissance valued individual human experience and traditional virtue. The present dawning of this new age presents a unique opportunity because it is an "age" still in formation, the fabric of values and ideals in which it will be clothed has not been completed. It is an age whose moral wardrobe remains up for grabs.

For this reason, we believe that today's business leaders are the single most influential group of individuals in our country. Where poets and playwrights shaped the Renaissance, and philosophers shaped the Enlightenment, business owners and leaders will shape this age.

The struggle to define the values and ideals that will be championed, encouraged, and rewarded by this age is at a critical juncture. Already the scales of value and virtue are being tipped in a perilous direction. The information, speed, and abundance that have been ushered in by this new age have also initially created a shift in our values and ideals. The aim and purpose of business has grown increasingly self-centered. The very point of existence of too many corporations has become personal enrichment. It seems clear that, at least for the moment, our culture has begun to esteem financial success over integrity.

It is a profound shift, and within the crucible of the free market, the effect has been the rise of companies led by dishonorable men and women. Prominent leaders and companies, encouraged by the current corporate culture, have pursued personal gain and corporate conquest at the expense of thousands of employees and consumers. The current corporate ideals place profit above purpose and winning above honor. Recently we have seen the fall of some of those leaders and their companies; most notably Enron, Arthur Anderson, Tyco, MCI WorldCom, and Martha Stewart.

The issue extends far beyond these giant companies. It is just as central to mid and small sized companies. The subtle but broad gap between corporate ideals and values and the personal ideals and values of a company's leader and its employees has created an unnatural schism in the very being of many American workers. For many, we check our personal ideals, values, and faith at our office doors.

We live with hearts divided.

So we see this then as the great and present battle: the battle for the hearts of today's business leaders. We have written this book because in our own careers and lives, and in our clients' lives, we recognize an unmistakable longing to live out a higher purpose.

The bible says that God has "set eternity in the hearts of men."[1] And that longing which is common to all of humankind, a longing for meaning and for purpose, develops out of that unavoidable, however faint, awareness of eternity which the Almighty has placed within each of our breasts. Our hope is that in contemplating the principles, anecdotes and thoughts which are contained within this book, business leaders and other readers will seek to understand their own labor within an acknowledgement of this longing. We hope too that they will consider anew the justification for and maintenance of their companies as it grows out of and is shaped by that longing. Most importantly, we pray that business leaders will be moved to view and care for their employees and customers from the humble position of a full awareness of

---

[1] Ecl 3:11

those employees' and customer's humanity, the whisper of the eternal within hearts, and the atonement of Jesus Christ upon the cross.

As corporate leadership has faltered, today's workforce has grown correspondingly more transient with each passing year. The gold watch, signifier of a career invested with a single company, is a virtual thing of the past; a quaint, even laughable token of an era departed. Employees move from company to company, even career to career at remarkable speed. A 5-year employee constitutes a seasoned veteran in most organizations. Why?

We believe that employee transience is a direct result of their longing for higher purpose and a greater point gone unfulfilled. Many of today's companies have failed to provide their employees with a common point to those employee's efforts. Instead the point of work for the overwhelming majority of today's workers has become simply to get as much as they can in exchange for as little work as they can offer. This is not a symptom of generational laziness or the byproduct of the demise of the American work ethic. This individualistic aim is not the heart's desire of today's employees, instead it is the inevitable result when today's companies do not offer any common, transcendent "point" to their employees' efforts. In the void of a higher purpose, each individual inevitably organizes their life and efforts around their own individual pursuit.

No doubt that is why we have detected an immense upwelling of desire within today's employees to be inspired by a true purpose, to sacrifice for that purpose, and to be honestly cared for. It is a desire borne out of the innate longing of their heart. It is a desire to nobly answer the question, "What's the point?" It is a desire to be well led.

Recently we took a break from our office and drove to a neighborhood ice cream shop. It was the type of shop that is newly popular and which has popped up all over. Customers dream up their own ice cream concoctions and the kid behind the counter mixes it together on a frozen marble slab right in front of you. It's great ice cream and the teenage young man who was mixing our orders that day was working hard. He was working alone in the shop, but he was hustling and it seemed to us he was doing a fine job.

After the young man had handed us our ice cream and we had paid, Jeff dropped a dollar in the tip jar that sat on the counter. The young man managed a thin grin of thanks and then, adopting a self conscious posture, he began to sing a rhyming song of tortured thanks. Along with the other customers, we politely listened to the young man's 30 second ballad. When he finished, there was a moment of silence and the small ice cream shop was filled with a collective embarrassment. We left the store reflecting on the worst jobs we had ever had.

The young man's half-hearted song is actually part of his company's policy, informally coined, "Hollar for a Dollar". It would be unfair of us to say that the campaign always produces the awkward and belittling effect we witnessed. To be fair, we have also seen it achieving its desired effect in a more exciting location, on a busy Friday night, with a gaggle of giggling High School aged employees singing to a packed store of tourist who are feeding dollar bills into the tip jar like it's a juke box.

At its root, the campaign is a "culture" piece, designed to introduce a fun and productive atmosphere as well as to encourage tipping which improves employee performance. It is not inconceivable that the company's owners read and were impacted by one of the recent popular business books on the value of bringing 'fun' back into the workplace.

Perhaps convinced that the "Fun" principle was just what their company needed, they followed a thought line that might have gone like this: "We need to help our employees create a fun and enlivened atmosphere that will engage, excite, and make an impression on our customers. We'll get the most out of our employees when they are having fun and we'll increase the rate at which our customers come back if they have fun with our employees."

Sounds great. Sounds cutting edge even. Unfortunately for this particular company, the embarrassment of the young man we encountered represents the rule rather than the exception. The end result of the "culture piece" is a young man compelled to humiliate himself every time someone gives him a dollar.

One basic definition of prostitution is, "the selling of one's abilities, talent, or name for an unworthy purpose." From our side of the ice cream counter it seemed more like a company prostituting its employee in the name of a 'fun atmosphere', than it did an effective culture piece.

With so many companies employing their people for the clearly unworthy purpose of 'increased profits', is it any wonder that employee transience is at an all time high?

That young man, like every employee must ask and answer the question, "What's the point?" Perhaps for him, it is to make enough money to pay for car insurance. Maybe it is to satisfy his father's requirement that he have a job. Whatever the answer, it is the answer that was necessary to compel him to go to work that day, to hustle his way through customers, including us, and to sing his silly song.

One day, he will either not be able to answer the question in a way that satisfies his soul, or he will discover that he is able to better answer it working somewhere else. On that day he will quit.

What is the point? It is the great itching question that for modern Americans begins to develop as a whisper sometime in adolescents and reaches an often paralyzing volume half way through college. The existential cliché develops in starker clarity for some more than it does for others. Likewise, the effect of the question, "What's the point", the quest for the answer, the doubly vexing quest for the meaning of the question itself, and ultimately the answer, creates a unique experience for each individual. The fact remains that all American workers ask the question and one way or another, it must be answered.

All human action follows human will. By the earliest of ages we are doing things and not doing things because we decide to do and not to do those things. Even at that tender age, we require personal justification for all of our decisions of will. We need a point.

At age 6 Matt met a neighborhood kid after school and hit him in the nose. He got into his first fist fight because the night before his dad had told him to. For Matt, the point of the fight was to win his father's approval.

In kindergarten, Jeff used his desk scissors to harvest a shock of his own hair which he then glued onto the self portrait he was diligently working on. The simple point of his self styling was to follow the teacher's instructions to the letter, making the portrait as "life-like as possible." Indeed.

Even if you are unable or unwilling to remember back to your kindergarten days, anyone who has spent time around 5 and 6 year olds realizes that even at that tender age, they have an innate need to understand the point in all that they do. That is why the "big point" starts getting deferred even as early as kindergarten. As kindergartners we are told that the point of any activity; from "Dick and Jane" to 123's, the point of kindergarten itself, is to get us ready for grade school. In 1st Grade they tell us we are in a ferocious push to get ready for the next level of academic intensity.....2nd grade! And so it goes.

The point of all of grade school we soon come to realize has been nothing more than preparation for a true trial in human misery, Junior High School. Mercifully, as awkward pubescents we are soon encouraged that our misery has a point, preparation for High School. It is in High School that we seem to finally be let in on the real point, a point which becomes a repeated message from parents, teachers, guidance counselors and friends: The point of High School, in fact the point of our entire education has been to prepare us for College. (Is it any wonder that at this realization many kids with no intention of attending college suddenly view their entire educational experience as a progressive and colossal waste of time?)

The point of college, 'To prepare us for work", is the last half truth in a long string of deferred points. By that time most of us have developed the discernment to finally see through it. Generally, unless we are studying to be doctors, lawyers, or scientists it is here that this marathon deferment of the question, "What's the point?" finally ends. It often happens within the first year of college and may be punctuated by a great existential exclamation of, "Ah, @#%&@#$% !".

The sudden evaporation of this elusive "point" which has been pursued since kindergarten prompts differing responses in each person.

Jeff was a freshman in college when the realization hit him. At the time he also owned a business with over 70 employees and was making six figures. He quit college and began his career full time.

Matt too was a freshman when the realization came. His response was to bury his head in the nearest bong, and lose all interest in school.

While Jeff's response was perhaps the more responsible, both of our experiences demonstrated our innate need to have a point to our efforts. Without a point to pursue both of us abandoned the endeavor.

The point of anything is nothing more or less than its purpose. The point is, in other words, the justification essential to any action or word. The point is the answer to both the simple and the great question, why?

For every action a "why" can be found. For every scratch, there is the itch that precedes it.

Nowhere has this fundamental human principle become more dramatically evident and yet more plainly ignored than in today's workplace. The great number of business leaders and the business thinkers which influence them will readily explore, trumpet, espouse and adopt any myriad of philosophies, systems, and programs aimed at increasing profit. They go to extraordinary lengths to understand and direct employee motivation. Yet for far too many business leaders the ultimate question of motivation, "What's the point" is viewed as an irritating and, ironically, a pointless query.

The fact is, without a point none of us will do anything. Ask the man who is running from a bear, what is the point of his running. He will have a ready answer - survival. Ask the miner digging in the dark, what is the point of his toil. He will tell you – reward. Ask the mother singing to her feverish child at 3 am, what is the point of her song. She will tell you – love.

These three great human motivations: Fear, Reward, and Love are no secret. The mastery of these basic motivators has been the well-spring of the vast majority of management theory.

The common thought line can be stereotyped like this: "I want my company to make more profit, and so I will scare, incentivize, or love my employees to achieve more profit." Aside from the obvious fallacy of calling manipulative kindness 'love', the central and enormous error of this train of thought is that its point is profits, and profits present little real benefit to workers.

Profit as a point unto itself is not a higher calling; it is a hollow chasing. It is not a transcendent purpose; it is common pursuit. It is not a collective endeavor; it is at best the collection of many individual efforts.

That is not to say that awareness and understanding of the 3 great motivators is corrupt in and off itself. The dynamic simply is. To ignore it would be foolishness. The problem is that nearly across the board, the 3 great motivators are applied to achieve the same empty and soulless point: more profits.

Fixation upon the desired result (profits) logically produces management systems and methodologies designed to maximize profitability. These management systems, theories and methodologies amount then to nothing more than well veiled manipulation. Offices may be collaboratively organized, meetings may be motivationally designed, management structure may be intentionally empowering, production minimums may be set, and Fridays can always be casual. The means may be soft and fuzzy, or hard and harsh, but the goal is always increased profits. No matter how compassionately or enlightened it is couched, the majority of management theory makes employees nothing more than the human sums of simple motivational equations.

It is from within this environment that we believe a stirring has begun. It is a stirring among the hearts of American workers and especially in the hearts of American business leaders. A desire is growing for something more; something different; something that matters.

What is beginning to happen in a few extraordinary companies, and what we pray will begin to happen more and more, is the development of businesses focused on purposes worth pursuing. It is these extraordinary companies which will radically revolutionize the corporate landscape, and Lord willing, the very landscape of our modern culture. These are companies that have a transcendent point, and it is a point worth chasing after. These are companies made up of employees who share a common purpose that supersedes their own individual purposes.

Over the last year we have had the good privilege of working directly with, observing, or studying several of these extraordinary companies. More and more of these wonderful, and very different, companies are popping up upon the landscape. In fact you may very well be the leader of, or in, one of them. For the purposes of this book we have identified three companies which we believe are worth noting and examining. Those three companies are Buffini and Company, SAS, and HomeBanc Mortgage Corporation.

In almost every facet, these are 3 very different companies - They are different sized (Buffini and Company has 200+ employees while SAS has 9000+); have different structures (SAS is the largest privately owned software company in the world while HomeBanc is publicly traded on the NYSE); and they operate and serve 3 completely different industries (SAS is a analytic software company, Buffini and Company is a business training and coaching company, and HomeBanc is a mortgage lender).

What these companies have in common however is what leads us to include them in this book. As we will see, that common ground is the deep and lasting impact that they have had in lives of their employees and customers and the extraordinary success that they can claim as a result. We will also see that these three companies are led by three individuals who have led these companies in pursuit of a purpose that is uncommon in these days, but which has made all the difference.

Periodically throughout this book we will refer back to Buffini and Company, SAS, and HomeBanc, letting the experiences of these businesses and their leaders provide an instructive example from an extraordinary company. Many of our readers may be familiar with these three companies. For those readers who are yet unfamiliar with the story of each of them, we are glad to introduce you.

Arriving from his native Ireland at the age of 20, Brian Buffini did not have a definite plan for his life in America. Soon a chance encounter would lead Brian into a career in the Real Estate industry. Drawing on the simple but profound wisdoms he had learned working for his family's painting business as a boy in Ireland, he developed and systemized a radically efficient referral-based business methodology. Brian quickly used his unique methodology to grow a multi-million dollar Real Estate practice, becoming one of the nation's most productive Realtors. He was still in his early twenties.

At the height of his success in Real Estate, Brian and his wife Beverly made a remarkable decision to take the road less traveled. Leaving the security and overwhelming success of his Real Estate career, he founded a start-up, Buffini and Company. Brian understood the significant, universal struggles that a life of sales presented to an individual and their family. His vision was simple: to share the tools, techniques and methodologies he had developed with others, that they might enjoy a richer and more balanced life. The purpose of Buffini and Company then was the same as it is today: "To impact and improve the lives of people."

In the less than 10 years since its founding, Buffini and Company has become the #1 Real Estate coaching and training company in America. Through the company's seminars, Brian has personally trained over 800,000 individuals. Buffini and Company currently coaches over 7000 professionals (including Realtors, Lenders, Stock Brokers, Financial Planners, and Insurance Agents). In an industry with an annual client retention rate that averages less than 20%, Buffini and Company's client retention rate is over 75% and climbing. Many of those clients are near fanatical in their appreciation for and devotion to the company. Testimonials documenting 200% and 300% increases in business revenues and family time are the expected rule rather than the exception. Within the industry, Buffini and Company represents the gold standard; occupying the most respected and credible position within the marketplace.

Buffini's company is not just revered by its clients. Buffini and Company is also deeply beloved by its employees. Brian and his brother Gary (Buffini and Company's President and COO) place an extravagant value on the overall health and well-being of their employees and their employees' families. Through innovative programs aimed at employee care and wellness, the company has reduced sick days by 14%. Buffini and Company is so loved by its people that those employees have become remarkably effective company evangelists. Recently, when the company needed to hire 14 positions, they had 2,400 personally referred, pre-qualified applicant resumes to choose from…without placing a single ad or job listing.

SAS was founded in 1976 by Jim Goodnight and John Sall and from the beginning they operated upon a simple but striking concept - If you treat employees as if they make a difference to the company, they will make a difference to the company. More than a pretty sounding core value to be written in a business plan, CEO Jim Goodnight has taken employee care to a remarkable level.

SAS employees work in an environment that fosters and encourages the integration of the company's business objectives with their personal needs. With enviable low employee turnover that has been consistently and significantly below the industry average, SAS reaps the rewards of employee loyalty and the benefit of the most talented minds in the software business. Programs and facilities at its Cary, N.C., world headquarters include two on-site childcare centers, a masseuse, putting green, first class dinning commons, an eldercare information and referral program, an employee health care center complete with company doctors and nurses, wellness programs, a 77,000 square-foot recreation and fitness facility, and many other work-life programs.

The company's work-life programs and unique corporate culture continue to receive accolades. For eight consecutive years, the company has been listed in the top 20 of Fortune's "100 Best Companies to Work for in America" and was inducted into the list's "Hall of Fame" in 2005. In addition, SAS has been listed by Working Mother as one of the 100 Best Companies for Working

Mothers 13 times. In October 2002, SAS' corporate culture was featured in a segment titled "The Royal Treatment" on CBS' 60 Minutes and more recently was featured as the Best Place to Work on the Oprah show.

HomeBanc places particular emphasis on their mission – "To enrich and fulfill lives by serving each other, our customers and community…as we support the dream of home ownership." Led by Patrick Flood the company, now publicly traded, is renowned for the remarkable culture that has been fostered around that mission and grown between employees.

In 2002 HomeBanc made a radical decision and hired a pastor in place of its HR Director. Pastor Ike Reighard was titled the Chief People Officer and the message was clear, HomeBanc truly sees their "Humans" as precious resources and the care and health of those employees is the company's first priority. Indeed the company's investor relations material plainly states, "HomeBanc believes its most valuable asset is its people."[2] The company history is filled with amazing stories, some of which we will explore later, of employees going to extraordinary lengths to care for each other and their clients.

SAS, HomeBanc, and Buffini and Company are three in a small but growing group of emerging extraordinary companies. They are companies that are well led. They are companies that are worth working for. They are companies in pursuit of a transcendent purpose. Throughout this book Buffini and Company, and other companies, will provide us with wonderful real world insight into the application of the principles that we explore.

---

[2] HomeBanc Corp. Investment Profile – August 2005

"You ask and do not receive, because you ask with wrong
motives, so that you may spend it on your pleasures" - James
4:3

The main concept that we hoped to convey in Chapter 1 is that every business
has a central point to its existence; a purpose towards which it endeavors.
"What's the point?" is the single most important question that a business
leader must answer within their business.

The leaders of extraordinary companies have boldly wrestled with and answered
this question. The point of existence for their companies is transcendent. It is
a higher purpose that is central to all that they do and all that they are. The
leaders and employees of these remarkable companies partake in that purpose,
and it becomes the point of their daily efforts. They share a "common unity"
of purpose, becoming quite literally a "community" that is wholeheartedly
dedicated to that purpose.

Regrettably, for the majority of businesses today, "What's the point" is a
question which has been largely ignored, its answer assumed. Most businesses
today do not have a transcendent point to their existence nor do they have a

higher purpose to their efforts. The point and purpose of most companies is in fact very ordinary – increased profits.

The effect of 'increased profit' as the purpose for the overwhelming majority of modern business is far reaching. The point and purpose of a business is also the motivation of every work day. In the eyes of the company it is necessarily the point and purpose of every employee's existence. The stark deduction is that when 'increased profit' is the purpose of a company, it is also that company's point and purpose for the hiring and care of its employees.

'Increased profit' becomes the unfortunate point of each employee and customer relationship. With profit as the central purpose of that relationship, authentic care within that relationship is impossible. The employee or customer is a tool used to achieve an objective and in such a dynamic it is always the object instead of the tool that is valued and cared for.

We are reminded of C.S. Lewis' striking allegory from *The Four Loves*:

> "We use a most unfortunate idiom when we say, of a lustful man prowling the streets, that he "wants a woman." Strictly speaking, a woman is just what he does not want. He wants a pleasure for which a woman happens to be the necessary piece of apparatus. How much he cares about the woman as such may be gauged by his attitude to her five minutes after fruition (one does not keep the carton after one has smoked the cigarettes)."

Although graphic, Lewis' classic quip is nonetheless a remarkably accurate parallel to the modern day workplace. For many companies it is neither an employee nor a customer that the company wants. In fact, the headaches, costs, and liability they associate with them make both the employee and the customer exactly what the company does not want. As the popular one-liner goes, "This would be a great business if it weren't for the customers." These companies want more profit. The employee and customer alike are no more than the "necessary piece of apparatus" required to achieve the company's desire.

There is a basic equation that can be constructed governing business and management thought. On the right side of the equation, is the answer to the question "What's the point". It is the purpose and motivation for the existence and efforts of a company. On the left side of the equation is the formula of business process and methodology which is developed in an effort to arrive at that value:

$$\frac{\text{(PROCESS AND METHODOLOGY)}}{} = \frac{\text{(PURPOSE AND MOTIVATION)}}{}$$

For the majority of businesses and business theorists, the assumed answer to the question, "What's the point," the right side of the equation, has remained the same: "INCREASED PROFIT".

$$\frac{\text{(PROCESS AND METHODOLOGY)}}{} = \frac{\text{INCREASED PROFIT}}{\text{(PURPOSE AND MOTIVATION)}}$$

The left side of the equation consists of the formula which is the subject of the theories and practices which have risen out of Business Schools, Board Rooms and business books over the years. The left side of the equation is the "How?" Top down, bottom up, team building, stock options, cost cutting, even servant leadership. Whatever the strategy is, it becomes the process which is formulated in an attempt to achieve the result on the other side of the equation: INCREASED PROFIT.

$$\frac{\text{BUSINESS PROCESS} + \text{STRUCTURE} + X}{\text{(PROCESS AND METHODOLOGY)}} = \frac{\text{INCREASED PROFIT}}{\text{(PURPOSE AND MOTIVATION)}}$$

So what is wrong with these equations? Is it naïve to call into question one of the most basic business refrains: "We are in business to make a profit"?

Generally accepted opinion inside and outside of the Christian Church is that it is simply the way of capitalism. Good men and women, and many of those of faith, have unapologetically conceded profit as the central point of existence for their business. The focus has been on the left side of the equation and not the right. Even for Christian business leaders, the most important question has not been, "What is the point", but rather "How do we get there?" It is perhaps the most common position taken by both Christian and non-Christian business leaders today. It seems that for many of us, 'increased profits' can remain the central purpose of our business so long as those profits are pursued in a manner that seems morally redemptive.

Executive Pharisees

This train of thought has opened the door to, and even encouraged the use of biblical Judeo-Christian principles as a means to achieve a business end. The regrettable result is often no more than a pimping of Christian principles and the Christian faith for worldly gain. It is an issue that extends far beyond the shameless printing of Christian fish symbols on business cards.

CHRISTIAN PROCESS + STRUCTURE + X	=	INCREASED PROFIT
(PROCESS AND METHODOLOGY)		(PURPOSE AND MOTIVATION)

In the passage from the book of James which we placed at the beginning of the Chapter, the apostle reminds us that it is our motives that matter,

> "You ask and do not receive, because you ask with wrong motives, so that you may spend it on your pleasures" - *James 4:3*

Some scholars have indeed suggested that the literal notion that James is conjuring is one of attempting to make God one's pimp and the object of desire one's whore.

In God's economy, motivation is the gold standard. The Sermon on the Mount, the widow's mite, the repentance of Zaccheaus, nearly every teaching of our Lord comes back to the heart and the motivation which naturally flows from it. A company's motivation is found in nothing less than its central point and purpose. That is why we must ask ourselves the question, "What's the point?" As Christian business leaders we must come to a true understanding of our own motivations. Why do I run this company? What is the purpose? Why does this company exist?

It is not enough to practice Christian principles, however diligently, out of wrong motives. When we do, we are no more than executive Pharisees, praying in the public square, making sure our offering makes a commotion as it clangs about the offering pan, and thanking God that He has made us different than our pagan competitors.

What should be clear is that for any Christian business leader the motivation for the existence and efforts of business should not be increased profit. After all, how can it be when at the most basic level 'increased profit' is really nothing more than 'more money'? It seems abundantly clear that no matter how "Christian" the methods utilized are, if more money is the motivation of a business, those "Christian" methods amount to nothing more than a modern day whitewashing of pharisaical tombs.

We feel that it is important at this point to clearly communicate that by no means do we eschew the realization of profits, even tremendous profits, in Christian run businesses. In fact, extraordinary profits are one of the more common byproducts of companies which are committed to a higher purpose. Profit can be a byproduct of the pursuit of a higher purpose and even can be part of the planned process in pursuit of that higher purpose, but it should never be the purpose and motivation itself.

For instance we may consider Buffini and Company's annual profit goal. Brian Buffini led the company to set the goal, in part to fund the company's ongoing empowerment project in Africa, and in part to be distributed to the employees. When we consider motivation, the distinction is simple enough. Buffini and Company's motivation and purpose is not the realization of profit. It is to "impact and improve the lives of people"; both in Africa and in their own lunch room. For Buffini and Company the motivation and purpose has nothing to do with increased profit. Rather, the increase in needed profits is simply a component in the process formula designed to pursue the company's purpose. When Buffini and Company employees are asked the question, "What's the point?" They have a ready answer, "To impact and improve lives."

Buffini and Company's equation is simple and profound:

$$\frac{\text{PROCESS} + \text{STRUCTURE} + \text{PROFIT}}{\text{(PROCESS AND METHODOLOGY)}} = \frac{\text{LIVES IMPACTED \& IMPROVED}}{\text{(PURPOSE AND MOTIVATION)}}$$

Motivation is all that matters. It is not profits that corrupt but instead profits as motivation which do. The bible does not say that money is the root of evil. Instead it is the love of money that is the root of all kinds of evil.[3]

Over and over again our Lord clearly communicates to us that motivation is His concern; that He sees past performance and into the very heart, "God sees not as man sees, for man looks at the outward appearance, but the Lord looks at the heart."[4]

---

[3] 1 Tim 6:10
[4] 1 Sam 16:7

The Hijacking of Servant Leadership

The centrality and effect of the issue of motivation within modern business is well illuminated when we examine one of today's most popular management theories: Servant Leadership.

Both inside and outside of the Christian community, much has been made regarding servant leadership as a management theory and business practice. The powerful principle of condescension has experienced a revival of sorts in the business community. Over the last 25 years there have been a slew of books written about Servant Leadership. In direct challenge to earlier, more autocratic styles of business leadership, the way of the servant has been identified as a cutting edge leadership methodology, trumpeted by no less than the country's best Business Schools, and validated by some of the world's most beloved companies.

It would be difficult for even the most secular of thinkers to make a convincing argument that anyone other than the person of Jesus is the original inspiration for servant-hood as a leadership style. For Christians all the more, the condescension of Christ provides not only a singularly perfect example of ultimate leadership, but it is also the literal context for the whole of our faith.

When viewed within the context of Jesus and His Church, the existence and effective operation of the principle of servant leadership cannot be denied. Before His mission to earth, the Chief Executive Officer of the Cosmos and all of creation, the self-existent and eternal King of Kings was due and given the constant honor and adoration of the millions of heavenly hosts assembled within the courts of heaven. His authority unquestioned and His power unlimited, King Jesus sat upon His throne reigning over our world and innumerable, sparkling and spectacular others far off in unmeasured space. And still, this King of Kings, eternal and majestic, departed His glorious throne, taking on the flesh of man, and the poor rags of a pauper.

23

This one and only High King came to serve. Thirty three years departed from his heavenly throne, on a night long ago, in a small upper room in the Middle East, the King of the Cosmos fastened a towel around His waist and stooping down, washed the filth from the feet of His disciples. The yearly growth, impact, and legacy of the Christian Church since that night some 2000 years ago staggers the mind.

The popularity of Servant Leadership as a management philosophy is a direct result of the foundational truth of its principles. The fruit of a business leader's true service is in fact extraordinarily predictable and wonderfully beneficial. We know unequivocally that a servant leader increases their authority and influence over their employees. We also know that employees of a servant leader increase in their trust, loyalty, respect, and personal esteem of the company and its leadership. Finally, we know that trust, loyalty, respect, and esteem directly and positively effects recruitment, retention, and productivity; which ultimately increase profit.

Is it any wonder that the power and the promise of the natural byproducts of Servant Leadership appeal to all kinds of business leaders and thinkers? What business leader would not like to increase their influence and authority within their organization? What business leader does not desire increased employee and customer loyalty? Is it any wonder that the natural effects of servant leadership appeal not only to the company leader whose authentic desire is to glorify Christ by imitation, but also to the company leader whose point, purpose, and motivation is increased profit?

Perhaps that is why the net effect of 25 years of Servant Leadership theory on modern business has been nearly undetectable. The moment that anything done in the name of Servant Leadership becomes a tool to increase goodwill and favor with employees, it becomes nothing more than vain performance. When service requires reciprocation, it becomes nothing more than basic obligation. Utilized as a tool to achieve increased profit, it becomes no more than crass manipulation.

It is often said by companies that they "practice servant leadership." It is incumbent upon us to remember that Jesus Christ did not play act his role as servant. He became the flesh and blood of a servant. The King of the Creation's stable born, homeless wandering, multitude feeding, foot washing, brutally tortured, and finally crucified life was not an actor's portrayal of servant hood; it was the complete and utter ***embodiment*** of servant hood. Even to the point of death.

So if we are to be imitators of Christ we cannot simply play act the role of servant, we are to be servants. It is not enough to practice servant leadership in 3 powerful ways each week. But play acting is all that we are doing when the ultimate point and purpose of our business is INCREASED PROFIT. The motivation for our serving is corrupted and has become nothing more than pimping the principles of the creator.

Servant Leadership cannot be faked or counterfeited, which may be the reason that, however popular a management theory, it has failed to have a transformative effect on modern business. The true test of the authenticity of Servant Leadership is in its motivation. Motivation flows from the very heart of the leader.

It comes to no less than this: Only a Leader with a servant's heart can be a Servant Leader.

That heart is the sole determining factor in answering the question, "What's the point?" The leader's heart determines the point, purpose, and motivation for the business and so it is the leader's heart which determines whether their company is ordinary or extraordinary.

The central point and purpose of a business, the very motivation for its creation and continuation, the motivation for the labor of its employees and the patronage of its customers is everything.

Before you go any further, we encourage you to begin to consider the question: What is the point of your business? If you are a leader and worker in someone else's business, what is the point of your labor? Take the time to ask God to search your heart and reveal truth to you. Honest wrestling with this question is an edifying exercise to enter into.

It is a remarkably difficult question for most of us to answer honestly. Praise God if the point of your business and the point of your labor is a transcendent purpose. However, the plain truth is that for most of us, the point of our businesses has been increased profit. Praise God too if He brings you to a realization of that truth. The Lord is able to change and refine our hearts and with them the purpose and motivation which flow out.

Let us abandon the Pharisaical practices of writing core values and mission statements which have every appearance of righteousness but which are far from reflecting our hearts. Core Values and Mission Statements have become so disconnected from reality that they are now rarely taken seriously. We are like the Kings of old who required their portrait artists to render images of surpassing beauty, no matter how inaccurate.

As Christian business leaders, if we understand the central purpose of our company to be its very motivation, are we not compelled to carefully examine that central point and purpose? Understanding that God sees beyond the activity, methodologies, and management theories and peers into the very heart of our business, should not that central point and purpose of our business be our most primary concern? Rather than brushing aside the question, "What's the point" and far from assuming its answer, should it not be the most important question that any business leader ask?

> *"Therefore if anyone is in Christ, he is a new creature; the*
> *old things passed away; behold, new things have come." – 2*
> *Corinthians 5:17*

Hopefully we have established that every company has a central purpose: the point of and motivation for all that the company is and does. Made paramount within the organization by its leader, the central point, purpose and motivation of a company is the determining factor in the activity, culture, character, and health of any business. That central purpose flows naturally from the heart of the business leader, and it cannot be faked or counterfeited. As we often say around our office, "It is what it is."

As we have noted, in today's business climate, the highest purpose of the vast majority of companies is ordinary and individual. It is centered around and exclusive to the company's founder and/or leader.

One of the inherent problems with such an individualized central point and purpose is that it is exclusive to the company's leader. Such a purpose cannot be shared or adopted by the rest of the organization. Take for instance the company whose highest purpose is to provide financial freedom to its owner. Can that company's employees be expected to integrate the company's highest purpose into their lives and make it their own? Of course not. In fact it is laughable to imagine the employee who, when asked, "What's the point of your work," would happily reply, "To make 'ol boss Stewart as absolutely rich as possible."

The natural effect of a highest purpose that cannot be integrated into the lives and careers of employees is the creation of an organization of employees who each bring their own individual highest purpose into the workplace. This is a fundamental necessity since each employee must have an abiding point and purpose to get up and go to work each day. They must have a point and purpose to do the work they do, and a point and purpose for the way they do it.

The intrinsic and inevitable result of every employee having a unique purpose is a company of individuals which has a natural inertia which tends towards dissonance and dissipation. The Lord says, "Every man's way is right in his own eyes."[5] The point and purpose of each individual determines the way they work. Each individual's 'way' flows from the pursuit of his or her individual purpose. The net effect is that for every 20 employees, there are 20 ways to do something.

In these ordinary companies, each employee at their desk, on the docks, or in the field would answer the question, "Why are you meeting, loading, or selling today" differently. It is the pension. The upside. The experience. The health benefits. For most, it is the money - the simple and authentic drive for provision. Because the highest purpose of the company is different from the highest purpose of its employees, the result is an organization of employees that must be cajoled and manipulated to achieve management's desired end.

---

[5] Proverbs 21:2

But what happens when the point and motivation of a company, its highest purpose, is transcendent? What happens when there flows from the heart of a leader a purpose, point and motivation which is bigger than that leader, beyond increased profit, and outside of the ordinary?

HomeBanc's Chief People Officer Ike Reighard is passionate about exploring that possibility. In a 2003 interview, shortly after joining HomeBanc, Reighard said, "To me, a job is too small to fill up a person's spirit. I want to help them find purpose in what they do, see the bigger picture of what we are trying to accomplish as an organization."[6]

As we will see, the natural effects of a transcendent highest purpose on the material success and health of a business are profound. As a result, exploring those remarkable effects on a company's culture, operations, and impact presents an inevitable catch 22: the extraordinary results, including financial, of a company pursuing a transcendent purpose would seem to offer ample justification for the adoption of such a transcendent purpose by every company; and yet to pursue the extraordinary results is to make the results the purpose and the transcendent idea nothing but a beautiful manipulation constructed to achieve those extraordinary results.

Under the eyes of God motivation is all that matters. We need only look at the company of Christ during His earthly ministry to discover this striking mandate. Jesus spent little time with the successful, respected, pious, phylactery wearing religious rulers of His time. Though they said the right things, scrupulously pursued the law, practiced their religion with tremendous zeal, and had the respect of their communities, our Lord knew their hearts and the selfish motivations that sprang from them. Instead Jesus led and lived among those whose hearts He had changed. He made brothers and apostles

---

[6] *"The Patriotic Recruiting Gospel of a Chief People Officer"*, Workforce Management, July 2003

out of the fishermen and tax collectors whose motivations transcended their own lives, lives that would be laid down in service of Christ.

A transcendent purpose then must be by definition pure. The central point and motivation of a company can only flow from the heart of its leader. It is simply authentic, or it is not.

When asked by "60 Minutes" about the oddity of treating SAS employees as wonderfully as they are treated, founder and CEO Jim Goodnight incredulously responded, "What's wrong with treating your people good?"

In many ways Goodnight's philosophy of employee care is complex, and yet in most ways it is remarkably simple. After all, what indeed is wrong with treating your people good? To a leader like Goodnight, there is no other option. It flows from who he is, and there has been no other choice for SAS since its founding in 1976.

When Brian Buffini founded Buffini and Company, the transcendent purpose of the company was, "To improve and impact the lives of people." What a wonderful purpose, isn't it? In these cynical times it may sound too wonderful, too simple, and too good. After all, there are hundreds of thousands of beautifully written but completely ignored mission statements all across the country. The difference was that this was the authentic purpose of Brian's heart. It was the justification and motivation for beginning the company. It was the point.

It is important to remember that a transcendent purpose is pursued within the real world. As a result, the pursuit almost always takes place upon the stage of the everyday. The purpose is transcendent, but its pursuit is often gritty, uncertain, tiresome, and disguised in the common clothes of the everyday.

The founding of Buffini and Company was no different. In the beginning the practicality of pursuing Buffini and Company's purpose felt far from transcendent. Brian was thought of and even called irresponsible and reckless. To many, leaving such a successful and lucrative business to begin a start-up seemed either insane, or incredibly egotistical. Indeed, in the company's early years, the scope of Brian's vision, "To impact and improve the lives of people," remained daunting to even he and his wife.

Patrick Flood has led HomeBanc from a relatively small mortgage originator to the owner of a ticker symbol on the New York Stock Exchange and a top 20 ranking on Fortune's 2005 Best Companies to Work for list by steadfastly adhering to a basic philosophy, "People first is the only way to build an extraordinary enterprise."[7]

Transcendent Purpose

A transcendent purpose is an objective beyond the individual leadership and outside of the company. It is a purpose which is not self-reflexive either for the individual leader or for the company. A transcendent purpose is always outwardly focused, must require sacrifice, and is intrinsically honorable. For the Christian business leader, the transcendent purpose of their company is a specific corollary to the purpose of their life: To glorify the Lord Jesus Christ.

From building a hospital in India to providing honest and reliable car repair, a transcendent purpose can be spectacularly splendid or disguised in the plain clothes of everyday. What matters is that it authentically flows from the heart of the leader and that the leader has established it as the ultimate and highest purpose of the company.

As an example, consider two local garages. The first exists to provide well for the owner and his family by delivering superior service at honest prices.

---

[7] *"HomeBanc Named #20 on Fortune Magazine's Best…"*, HomeBanc Press Release, January 10, 2005

This business has an ordinary purpose, not a transcendent one. Although the means to achieve that purpose are good and right (delivering superior service at honest prices), the purpose of the company is still, "to provide for the owner" which is intrinsically self-reflexive.

In contrast is the garage across town whose highest purpose is maintaining the safety and utility of the vehicles of their beloved clients. This garage does have a transcendent purpose. The purpose is not self-reflexive. The owner's family is provided for as a necessary result, but it is not the purpose. The purpose is clearly outwardly focused and when examined it is also sacrificial. Consider the client that arrives at closing with car trouble. The family requires the car for the father to get into work the next day. To pursue their purpose the owner or an employee must sacrifice their time, staying late into the night to get the vehicle fixed. Finally, although simple, such an authentic purpose of true service and client care is an honorable one, and, most importantly, it is to the glory of Christ.

Is this splitting hairs? Is there any benefit in zealously examining the purpose and motivation for a business and its leader?

The inescapable fact remains that our companies exist and operate within the material world. The preeminence of motivation in the eyes of God is not a principle that evaporates in the workplace. On the contrary, it is within the material world that our motivations are tested, revealed, and refined.

Transcendent Purpose and the Individual

Before we examine the enormous material effects of a transcendent purpose on a company, it is profitable to consider the effect of a transcendent purpose on an individual. For each Christian, simply considering our own testimonies and the testimonies of our brothers and sisters provides the most compelling evidence for the dramatic and overwhelming effect of a transcendent purpose on an individual life. When the Christian dies to themselves and is spiritually reborn into new life in Jesus Christ, that new life has an ultimate and transcendent purpose. No longer self-involved, self-gratifying, and self-pursuing, the Christian dies to their old self and to their ordinary, fleshly points and purposes for life; raised to new life as a new creation.

That new creation has a heart that is fixed on a singular, transcendent point and purpose. Rick Warren wrote one of the most popular Christian books of the decade, "The Purpose Driven Life" on this very subject. The singular and central purpose, point and motivation for all of life is the Glory of Christ. The lifelong pursuit of that transcendent purpose produces testimonies and stories which, in their splendor, over and over testify to the power of Christ and the perfection of His purpose.

Consider the length to which everyday believers go and are called to go in pursuit of Him and His purpose. We have a friend who ran the local Young Life mission in San Diego County for 10 years. He often refers to the work of the Lord as "chasing after God." Leon left a 7 figure career as a currency trader in New York to pursue the highest purpose of His heart, leading a chase after the hearts of teenagers.

What could lead a man to move his family across the country, across socioeconomic strata, and into the harrowingly uncertain world of teen outreach ministry? Could it be the same thing that compelled a millionaire Real Estate professional to walk away from his career and found a company with the expressed purpose to, "Impact and improve the lives of people"? Or the same impulse which led Jim Goodnight to open Montessori day care centers for the 850 children of his employees, on the SAS campus.

"Seek ye first the kingdom of God and His righteousness…[8]" the profundity of that beautiful scripture expands evermore when we encounter in our own

---

[8] Matthew 6:33

lives and in the lives of others the reality of a heart fixed on the singular and transcendent purpose that is Jesus Christ.

Consider the workers associated with Wycliffe Bible Translators and the bible translation movement at large. Many of these men and women of faith labor in the world's most isolated villages, some for over 20 years, to bring the Word of God to remote people groups. What if we were to contemplate the work of these men and women from a completely secular point of view?

What would compel a couple to lead their family into such a journey? What would urge them to leave their home and their homeland? To sell their earthly possessions? To say goodbye to friends and extended families? To leave their earthly security and the cradle of unprecedented American abundance? To go knowing their journey may take 10, 20, even 30 years?

They move to a completely foreign, often primitive, and sometimes hostile culture. They do this to live immersed within a foreign people, to painstakingly learn and document the language and the history and meaning behind each word. For some, the initial years may be spent developing the first standardized written form of the language and then teaching that written form back to the culture. After that momentous task, they will labor years and years more, meticulously translating every word of an ancient religious text, originally written thousands of years ago by a vastly different culture.

What would compel a family to such a journey? What would keep them still fastened to the endeavor 15 years into it and facing hardship and persecution? What would pull them on through the doubt, despair, loneliness, and fatigue of a 20 year mission? Certainly not money, for the work does not pay. Not security, for earthly security is ultimately abandoned in the journey. Not fame, for the cultures are remote and anonymous. Only a transcendent purpose – a purpose above all others; divine, honorable, and ultimate could justify such a reckless pursuit.

The pursuit of such a purpose can ultimately only be defined, energized, and undertaken through the empowering singular purpose and person of our Lord Jesus Christ. The simple transcendent purpose of these missionaries labor is to bring the glorious, life giving Word of God Almighty to an entire people and culture. It is a corollary to the purpose of their lives.

From the mountains of Peru, to the deserts of North Africa, and the jungles of the Amazon, this purpose is being pursued all around the world. People from both outside of and from within these diverse cultures daily demonstrate the staggering effect of an authentic transcendent purpose in their lives.

This story from Wycliffe's 2003 annual report is particularly powerful, although not unusual:

> Kaka grew up as a shepherd boy. It was a hard life with few comforts, but through it he learned strength and endurance, along with gentleness and patience.
>
> For 16 years, Kaka worked on the translation of the New Testament in his language. During four of those years, he was leading believers as they went through much persecution. He spent two-and-a-half of those 16 years locked away in prison.
>
> Their New Testament came at a high cost. To Kaka, it was a price worth paying. During the many stages of drafting, checking and reviewing, he walked 6,000 miles in and out of the mountains. For a book of 1,000 pages, that's six miles per page. For every three pages he spent one night in the open, out on the trail, miles from home. And, for each page, the people of his village spent six-and-a-half days in prison, 18 man-years in all.
>
> Because of Kaka's faith, courage and tenacity, today there are hundreds of believers. Many have suffered unspeakably, some

at the hands of officials, others at the hands of revolutionary insurgents. His own son was arrested by the police, taken down to the river and shot 12 times with a high-powered rifle at point blank range. Kaka's nephew suffered the same fate, as have four other believers.

Kaka's heart was broken. Still, "God has called us as a tribal church to fill up the sufferings of Christ," he used to say, "and we will be faithful to the end."[9]

Dare we imagine an employee, or an entire company of employees who would pursue the purpose of their company with this type of passion? Unfortunately it may seem absurd at best and bordering on blasphemous at worst to consider this level of abandon and commitment within a modern company. Why? Does our Lord really expect less from our day-to-day lives than He does from the 'more spiritual' lives we unveil at Sunday Service, church retreats, and morning devotionals?

Leaving that contemplation for a moment, let us examine the effect of a transcendent purpose on one other man's life. Outside of Christ Himself, the Apostle Paul's life and words provide one of the singular greatest illustrations of the effect of a transcendent purpose.

Threatened with death by his Roman captors, Paul's response would essentially have been, "Great! To die is gain, for I'll be with my Lord."[10]

If instead the Romans had threatened to keep Paul alive and imprisoned in order to deprive him of that joy, his response would have likely been, "Fantastic! To live is Christ! So, let me live!"[11]

---

[9] Taken from Wycliffe Bible Translators, Inc. 2003 Online Annual Progress Report

[10] Philippians 1:21

[11] ibid

Confounded and angered at Paul's invincible joy, the Romans may have declared, "We will torture you, Paul."

"Be my guest," Paul essentially would have replied. "For I am sure the sufferings of this present time are not worthy to be compared with the glory that's coming!"[12]

The passion of Paul for Christ was the purpose of Paul's heart. It overwhelmed him, instructing his every word, step, and deed. Where the point of Saul's pious old life and legalistic ways had once been individual, self-righteous, and self-gratifying, Paul had a transcendent point and purpose with his new life that led him to be poured out for the body, humble, and self-sacrificing.

Indeed, Christians face and endure all manner of trial and struggle. All are called to sacrifice and some will indeed give all, their very lives for the one transcendent purpose of their hearts. That purpose is the glorious, everlasting, and ever noble purpose of being in the service of the King of Kings, the returning Prince of Peace, Jesus Christ.

Is it any wonder that, with such a majestic purpose embedded in our hearts, laboring for an ordinary and earthly purpose would leave our hearts wanting? After all, each of us as Christians has received a literal heart transplant. The Lord says, "Moreover, I will give you a new heart and put a new spirit within you; and I will remove the heart of stone from your flesh and give you a heart of flesh."[13] That new heart is an eternal heart and it has a transcendent purpose that has been hardwired into it by the Lord Himself. The highest purpose of our new heart is the glorification of Christ. Any attempt to subjugate that divine purpose with an ordinary earthly one, like increased profit, causes a profound discomfort at the deepest level of our existence. An unnatural schism is created when any purpose, no matter how well conceived,

---

[12] Romans 8:18
[13] Ezek 36:26

37

is pursued in competition to the divine and transcendent purpose that a believer's new heart is hardwired for.

The result of introducing a competing purpose is anxiety, unhealth, guilt, and disorder. The old Autopia ride at Disneyland in Anaheim, CA provides us with an excellent analogy. For a young child, the ride's allure is obvious and absolutely outstanding: the opportunity to drive their own car! Gas power, a seat belt, an actual accelerator, and most importantly, a real steering wheel.

What the youngest of children do not realize is that there is a steel rail running down the center of the track which absolutely determines the ultimate direction of each and every little car. The young motorist can steer left or right no more than two feet off course before the rail provides an immovable directional boundary. No matter what, the direction and destination of the car and its 'driver' is determined. The illusion of self-determination begins and may remain complete for young boys and girls, but the reality of the steel rail remains fixed.

The resulting experiences on the Autopia are predictable and instructive. For the kindergarten-aged motorists who remains unaware of the absolute imperative of the steel rail, their journey down the track is punctuated by abrupt, wild turns of the steering wheel. Biting their lip with determination they spin the wheel first right, then left as the car slams back and forth into the steel rail. Still the car continues on its course, however bumpy, guided by the rail.

For the young driver who, halfway through the experience begins to deduce the inevitability of the rail's influence on their course, a frustration often develops.

"What a gip!" the kid thinks as they come face to face with the fact that no matter how hard they turn the wheel their ultimate course is out of their hands.

The frustration, mixed with an inevitable curiosity, causes many a young Autopia motorist to throw their hands up in exasperation and surrender. Keeping their foot on the gas the immediate result is a remarkably uncomfortable ride as the car bounces even more spastically along the rail, making its inevitable way down the path.

It is at this point that fresh opportunity to enjoy the experience arises. If they retake the wheel, the young driver will realize they can steer freely upon the path laid out, so long as they keep the rail centered beneath the car. The result is an exhilarating challenge for the youngster, carefully steering in the direction laid out by the rail before them; they drive as absolutely best they can to keep from bumping into the rail, making the ride as smooth and enjoyable as possible.

As Christians the divine and transcendent purpose within our hearts acts like the rail at the Autopia ride; it determines our direction, as well as, thanks be to God, our final destination. As Christian business leaders we can still, and many do, thrash the wheel left or right in pursuit of other ordinary purposes, but we always eventually meet the jarring, unmovable reality of His ultimate purpose. Likewise, we can try and avoid the leadership role which God has called us to altogether; in essence taking our hands off the wheel. We will find soon enough that the ride is all the more bumpy and uncomfortable, but that our course somehow returns us over and over to the path of leadership. In the end the imperative is courageous leadership which submits to, pursues passionately, is directed by, and is according to that single transcendent purpose which God has placed within our heart.

As believers in Christ, because the purpose that flows from our hearts has been supernaturally rewired – it is not a purpose that we can cultivate, cajole, or create. Instead it is imparted wholesale to us. And just as we cannot manufacture it, we can also not escape it. After all, despite his best efforts to the contrary, Jonah did eventually preach in Nineveh.[14]

---

[14] "Then the LORD commanded the fish, and it vomited Jonah up onto the dry land." - Jonah 2:10

Understanding that an authentic transcendent purpose can only flow out of a rightly motivated heart, let's consider the natural results of such a transcendent purpose on a company's health, stability, culture, and yes, bottom line.

The Tripod of a Successful Company

If today's companies are indeed stages, then each of those stages is supported by three simple and fundamental components. Like a tripod, each component is an essential leg in the stability of the company. The three fundamental components of a company's success are:

1. Recruitment
2. Retention
3. Productivity

Every issue, from branding to employee benefits, tax credits to product development, site maintenance to EBITDA, falls under the heading of one of these 3 basic business issues. Consequently, these three fundamental components (we'll call them RRP for short) have always been and continue to be the abiding focus of all business leaders.

These three fundamental issues are best expressed as three simple questions. They are the three bedrock business questions of every company leader:

> 1. How do we attract more of the right employees and customers? (Recruitment)

> 2. How do we keep those employees and customers? (Retention)

> 3. How do we maximize the productivity realized in our relationships with those employees and customers? (Productivity)

On the broadest scale these three components determine the health, stability, and success of every business. When these three legs are solidly established, stable, and secure the company platform can become an extraordinary stage for the exploration of success, significance, and legacy.

When understood within the simple context of these three questions, the task of leadership is relatively straight forward. The sole and simple requirement is to lead a company to **the practice of consistently answering the three bedrock business questions well.**

Evidence of this simple truth is readily evident. After all, any company which is effectively attracting new customers and employees, retaining the ones it already has, and maximizing the productivity of employees, operations and assets is a truly successful company, and is probably also a world-beater.

Regardless of whether a company has an ordinary or a transcendent purpose, successfully addressing RRP is inevitably correlated with the successful fulfillment of that purpose.

Each of the three fundamental business questions poses their own unique and extraordinary challenges. For any business, answering just one of them well is a significant accomplishment. Answering one does not, however, create a successful business.

Consider the business that excels at Recruitment. Proficient at "getting people in the door" (lead generation, customer origination, and new employee recruitment) but lacking a culture of service or product excellence to retain those customers and employees, it is a company with a severely leaky bucket. Such a company has answered one of the three questions well. If that is all that it does it will soon fail.

Jeff was reminded of an afternoon spent as a 12 year old standing outside the entrance to a local country club, hawking candy bars for a school fund-raiser to the members. Making his pitch to a particular older gentleman who was shuffling his way into dinner, Jeff was kindly waved off.

"Sorry son," said the man, before pulling open the entrance door, "I'm a diabetic. I can't have sugar."

"Wonderful, sir," young Jeff retorted as he held up one of the candy bars, "It says right here, '100% Pure Milk Chocolate!'"

Stopping in his tracks the gentleman began to chuckle, "Oh, that's beautiful," he said turning back to Jeff. "Here's a dollar. You can eat the candy bar son."

The chocolate company had identified the perfect sales force for its product - children. Abundant, energetic, free, cute, and direct, the eyes of a child make them exponentially more difficult to walk past than a candy rack. Combined with their clear fundraising metrics and the compelling value propositions offered to schools and other organizations, the chocolate bar company had customer recruitment down to an art.

Their ability to retain those customers was another matter. After all, its a stretch to imagine the customer who, upon eating the candy bar, thought, "Wow, what an incredible $1 chocolate bar! I think I'll track down the company and order a couple more." Even repeat customers had to be recruited again and again.

Productivity remained a significant issue as well. The promise of being entered in a raffle to win a BMX bike loses a considerable degree of its shine for the average 12 year old kid after they have wasted 4 hours of their Saturday in front of a supermarket door.

Wonderful at answering the Recruitment question, but lousy at answering the Retention and Productivity ones, the chocolate bar company of Jeff's youth has slowly gone by the wayside.

The effective leader has built and maintains a successful business through the consistent practice of answering all three questions simultaneously. Indeed, nearly all of the management and business theories we have alluded too are aimed at successfully answering these three bedrock questions. And to be fair, many of the current business systems and theories do provide the tools to successfully address Recruitment, Retention, and Productivity.

Still, these theories and systems target Recruitment, Retention and Productivity in various ways as a means in pursuit of an ordinary highest purpose: increased profits. In pursuing an ordinary highest purpose, RRP become the necessary building blocks which are the determining factors in the fulfillment of that ordinary point and purpose. When a company's highest purpose is increased profits, the successful development of RRP is the natural determining factor in the successful pursuit of those profits. Inversely, when the company's highest purpose is transcendent, the pursuit of that purpose is the natural determining factor in the successful development of RRP.

Transcendent Purpose and the Employee

Remember that a transcendent purpose is an objective beyond the individual leadership and outside of the company. It is a purpose which is not self-reflexive either for the individual leader or for the company. A transcendent purpose is always outwardly focused, requires sacrifice, and is intrinsically honorable. For the Christian business leader, the transcendent purpose of their company is a specific corollary to the purpose of their life: To glorify the Lord Jesus Christ.

One of the fundamentally transformative effects of a transcendent purpose on a company is the adoption of that purpose by the company's employees. As we noted previously, an ordinary purpose is exclusive to the leadership, and by its very nature cannot be shared by the employees. Contrastingly, a transcendent purpose is not only available to, but encourages an authentic adoption of itself within the entire company.

As we have discussed, every individual employee requires a highest point and purpose for their efforts. Because a transcendent purpose is by definition adoptable, its effect is the migration of a company's population from a collection of individual employees with individual purposes to a community of co-laborers pursuing a common purpose. This unifying effect has far reaching and radical impact.

The employee who joins a company with a transcendent purpose generally does so with at least a basic understanding of and an appreciation for the company's purpose and its resulting culture. In fact, as we will see, the transcendent purpose is what these companies recruit employees to. The newly hired employee gradually progresses through 3 phases of assimilation into the company culture:

> 1. **Indoctrination:** Simply a comprehensive education into the transcendent purpose of the company, as well

as the Core Values, Fundamental Principles, Policies and Procedures, and contextual company history which support that purpose.

The goal of indoctrination is to provide the new employee with an opportunity to intellectually apprehend the point and purpose of the company.

2. **Integration:** This is the process of personal adoption which takes place generally over a period of months. It is the tangible, experiential participation in the pursuit of the transcendent purpose within the company's culture.

The goal of integration is the 18 inch migration of the transcendent purpose from the head to the heart. Integration is successful when the transcendent purpose supplants any individual purpose as the highest point and purpose for the employee's daily labor.

3. **Investment:** This is the natural result of the integration of a transcendent purpose. It is the inevitable and joyful expenditure the employee's best – from their hands, head, and heart in pursuit of the transcendent purpose.

The goal of investment is the authentic, independent, and personal ownership of the purpose by the employee.

Transcendent Purpose and Recruitment, Retention and Productivity

Finally, in full view of the effect of a divine and transcendent purpose upon the life of the individual, let's examine its impact on a company. As we will see, the positive impact of a transcendent purpose upon the Recruitment, Retention, and Productivity of a company is beyond extraordinary.

Here's why:

RECRUITMENT - Attracting more of the right employees.

1. **Purpose resonates purely and clearly.**
   A transcendent purpose strikes a harmonic chord which becomes the frequency of the entire organization. Remember that God has set eternity in the hearts of all[15]. That seed of the eternal produces a common longing for meaning and purpose. The authentic chord sounded by a company pursuing a transcendent purpose resonates with the eternal seed within the hearts of potential employees. A transcendent purpose attracts those potential employees at the most authentic and lasting level, ensuring that the company is not just attracting employees but is attracting the right employees.

2. **A culture of purpose attracts.**
   A group of individuals united in pursuit of a true transcendent purpose is overwhelmingly attractive. There is not a boy or man of any age who does not admire and occasionally fantasize of being part of a crack commando team in the U.S. Military. Firehouses and squad rooms hold a similarly powerful ability to attract the hearts and minds of us all. The individuals who belong to a culture of purpose are

---

[15] Ecl 11:1

easy to pick out. They have an attractive rest and confidence
that comes with a deeper certainty that their lives are 'on
purpose'.

A company with a transcendent purpose inevitably develops
a culture of purpose, producing employees who share an
understanding that their daily work and labor is 'on purpose'.
It is a company atmosphere and an employee characteristic
that captivates the hearts and minds of everyone around. A
culture of purpose is a culture people want to join.

3. **Authentic teams offer authentic belonging.**
    God made all of us for fellowship and for belonging. The
    team experience is one of the most productive and rewarding
    community fellowship experiences in human life. There are
    probably more business productivity theories and books on
    'team building' than any other business subject. Still, no
    matter how you try and build a team, how you support or
    motivate it, a team is only as strong as the team member's
    commitment to the common purpose.

    That is why one of a coaches most important jobs is leading
    his or her team into an understanding of their opponent.
    It is also why the ordinary purposes of a company need to
    be continually refined, tweaked, defined, and redefined
    in an attempt to continually provide new justification for
    commitment to the common purpose.

    In contrast, pursuit of a transcendent purpose gives rise to
    an authentic team, yoked together in a worthy and clear
    endeavor. The fellowship and belonging that such an
    authentic team offers is a powerful asset to recruit employees
    into.

4. **Purpose is a currency of ultimate value.**

A great deal of recruiting comes down to the 'package' that a company is able to offer prospective employees. Pay rate, salary, upside, pension, vacation, and benefits are all tallied in actual and hypothetical U.S. dollars. The prospective employee does their best to weigh on the other side of the scale such intangibles as schedule, drive time, travel, opportunity for advancement, personal relationships and basic company culture. U.S. currency, against the positives and negatives of the intangibles, becomes the measuring weight. A dollar is worth a dollar.

A company with a transcendent purpose has a rare currency over and above U.S. Dollars with which to recruit – the currency of purpose. Offering a prospective employee the opportunity to be a part of something significant, meaningful, and lasting – something eternal, creates an extraordinary advantage over competing suitors. For most, the currency of purpose has a value that they will not trade for the U.S. Dollar.

Buffini and Company has a photograph which they often show in presentations of one of their HR executives sitting behind a stack of fresh resumes which is literally two feet high. The company is relatively small, with just over 200 hundred employees, and yet they receive literally thousands upon thousands of resumes every year, without placing a single help-wanted solicitation.

SAS and HomeBank are no different. In fact, it is precisely for that reason that they both rank in the top 20 of Fortune's Best 100 and as a result are two of the countries most desirable companies to work for.

HomeBanc CEO Patrick Flood says, "In today's service economy, business success is driven by culture – having the right people who are thrilled to come to work each day, who are committed to the mission and who are trained for success produces extraordinary outcomes."[16]

RETENTION - Keeping those employees.

1. **A transcendent purpose is an irreplaceable distinctive.**
   We have established that every employee who gets up in the morning and goes to work must have a point and purpose to getting out of bed and going into work. The majority of employees work for companies which do not have a transcendent purpose and so the point and purpose of their workday is individual. They work to pay bills, to feed the family, or for benefits. Whatever it may be, that's the point.

   For these employees, fulfilling that point and purpose is what matters most. Their employers retain them by each day being the mechanisms by which those employees fulfill their point and purpose. For the great majority of workers, that point and purpose can be quantified in U.S. dollars. The result is that the employee can fulfill their point and purpose for getting up and going to work at any number of employers. If their point and purpose is provision, the employee can and probably will leave the company as soon as that point and purpose is better satisfied somewhere else. This is the very reason employee transience is at its highest mark.

   However, for the company with an authentically transcendent purpose their employees have adopted, integrated and begun to invest in the purpose of the company. They have independent ownership of the transcendent purpose and it is now the highest purpose for their individual work. It is a

---

[16] *"HomeBanc Named #20 on Fortune Magazine's Best…"*, HomeBanc Press Release, January 10, 2005

purpose which they cannot easily fulfill anywhere else.

2. **The pursuit of purpose is deeply satisfying.**

   Throughout all of human history, families have settled and communities have grown up around water. In Old Testament times the digging of a successful and productive well was paramount to settling a family or tribe in one place. So long as the well was wet, or the river was running, a family would settle, and begin to put down roots, building a life, a home, and a legacy in that place.

   The human heart thirsts deeply for meaning and divine purpose. One of the reasons that employees seem to wander from employer to employer is that their thirst for meaning remains unquenched. The corporate landscape has become somewhat of a desert and its employees nomads. When a company offers its employees a transcendent purpose, that company becomes like a well or a river. Its employees will drink deeply from that purpose and they will begin to settle, put down roots, build a life, a home, and a family around that company.

3. **Duty and honor.**

   The obligation that is implied in the words 'duty and honor' make many business leaders shy away from them for fear of scaring off their employees. In the current climate most employees are asked for little or no commitment. Managers are cautious not to spook employees, carefully avoiding words with connotations of commitment, such as loyalty, duty, and honor. Instead a message akin to, "so long as you meet your numbers and abide by our policies and procedures, everything is okey-dokey," has become common.

It's no surprise given the current landscape. After all, how can the highest and most noble human attributes of loyalty, duty, and honor be inspired or appealed to by an organization which exists for nothing more high or noble than making money?

In the company with a divine and transcendent purpose, the purpose itself intrinsically appeals to the highest and most noble attributes of the employees. In integrating the transcendent purpose into their own lives, the employees' pursuit of that purpose is both duty and honor bound. For the employees of these companies, to consider another job now requires consideration of their duty and honor and their commitment to the transcendent purpose which exists outside of the company itself. The individual has become more than a company employee and is now a partaker, investor, and integral part of that greater purpose to feed the community's elderly, modernize a village, fund a church building, keep the neighborhood's cars running, build a hospital, or whatever the transcendent purpose may be.

In the "60 Minutes" feature done on SAS, a long time employee is asked about his future at the company. After contemplating the question his response was simple, definitive, and resolute. "I can't imagine leaving SAS…if somebody offered to double my salary I wouldn't even think about it."

In an industry that typically sees annual employee churn in the 20% range, SAS employee turnover is at a staggeringly low 3% annually. It is important to keep in mind as well that SAS offers no stock options or other vesting equity incentives to retain its employees.

PRODUCTIVITY - Maximizing the productivity realized in our relationships with those employees.

1. **Sacrifice is volunteered.**

   The company that has a transcendent purpose has a
   community of employees which have adopted and integrated
   that highest purpose into their own lives and hearts. They
   share that purpose in common and it is the motivation
   for their labor each day. The Bible is clear that we are to,
   "Work as unto the Lord." The impact on the productivity of
   a community of workers who are pursuing a transcendent
   purpose together cannot be overstated. These employees will
   rightly offer their best labor as a sacrifice unto the common
   purpose. For the employee their productivity is uncoupled
   from their paycheck and instead linked directly to the impact
   it has on the pursuit of the purpose.

   At HomeBanc there is an "Associate Emergency Fund" which
   is funded solely by other HomeBanc employees and designed
   especially for employees who are facing extraordinary needs
   such as unforeseen medical bills, emergency travel, and other
   unexpected circumstances.

2. **Exchange rate is transformed.**

   Most of today's employees (those employed by companies
   with ordinary purposes) each have an individual and unique
   equation in their heads which governs the amount of work
   that they do in exchange for the compensation that they
   receive. They have arrived at what they believe is the 'fair'
   amount of attention, energy, and effort which can be expected
   from them (and which they expect from themselves) in
   exchange for the paycheck they receive.

   That individual equation is radically changed when the
   employee joins a company with a transcendent purpose. That
   transcendent purpose becomes their own and the 'exchange

rate' which they have used all of their careers to account for the amount of effort and energy they spend suddenly isn't correctly calibrated.

The question is no longer, "How hard must I work to earn my paycheck." It becomes, "How hard must I work that so that one kid can go to camp." The value of a transcendent purpose constrains its partakers to give their best in the effort of its pursuit.

3. **Purpose cultivates peace and health.**

   Peace and health directly correlate to worker productivity. The most productive workers are peaceful and healthy. Clearly, sick employees and sick days wreak havoc on productivity and an improvement in employee health has remarkable effects on a company's bottom line. But, what about peace? What is employee peace and how does it effect productivity?

   Peace and health are intertwined. The cause of sick employees and sick days is illness, or disease. The word disease can be broken into two parts. The first part, 'dis' means, "to separate or remove". The second part 'ease' means literally, "peace". So 'disease' actually means a separation or removal from peace. Peace is a transcendent quality of the heart. So it is no surprise then that stress, frustration, anger, and sadness; things that cause dis-ease in a life, have a direct impact on physical health.

   The pursuit of transcendent purpose then, one which satisfies the heart, ushers peace into the lives of employees. The job becomes more than the car, the office, the desk, the computer, the phone, and the car again. It takes on an abiding eternal significance and that purpose brings peace to the heart. That peace brings health, and healthy at peace employees are extraordinarily productive.

4. **It's a family affair.**

Finally, there is simultaneously no greater asset and no greater threat to worker productivity than the worker's family. A spouse and family which resent the work of the employee can have a devastating effect on productivity. Hours, concentration, and enthusiasm can all suffer dramatically.

On the contrary, the family which believes in the work of the employee can much more easily join with that employee to take a team approach to the work. The family that is able to share in a meaningful purpose with the employee can become a tremendous asset to that worker's productivity, giving that worker 'permission' in a sense to give themselves wholly to their work while they are there.

The story of HomeBanc includes the story of a loan officer sticken by cancer, and the story of the colleagues around him that came to his aid and supported him and his family through his recovery. As a company HomeBanc met his family's need. Meanwhile, voluntarily, his co-workers put deals of their own in his pipeline so that throughout his entire recovery his family was fed. As CEO Flood has said, that type of culture has extraordinary consequences.

SAS is convinced (and in fact they design the analytical software tools to quantify the impact) that their way of doing business – 35 hour work weeks, no stock options, day care on campus, an internal medical and nursing staff, gourmet lunch room, putting green, and masseuse to name a few – has greatly increased worker productivity.

Clearly the natural effects and byproducts of an authentic transcendent purpose on a company's RRP are extraordinary. The resulting impact on such a company's health, stability, culture, and, bottom line is also extraordinary. A company with a transcendent purpose is a company set apart, pursuing a purpose which cannot be captured on the bottom line; yet realizing a bottom line that cannot be achieved pursuing anything else.

*Whatever you do, work at it with all your heart, as working for the
Lord, not for men, since you know that you will receive an inheritance
from the Lord as a reward. It is the Lord Christ you are serving.* -
Colossians 3:23-25

The Origin and Purpose of Work

Perhaps a reality check is in order. Thus far we have begun to explore concepts
and ideals which appeal to the noblest parts of our humanity – transcendence,
honor, unity, sacrifice, and service. Does our daily work, the most mundane
and common activity of our lives, truly warrant such a meditation? Are
we taking ourselves and our labor too seriously? Do we risk elevating the
mundane and the secular to the level of the sacred?

For professionals today, a biblical understanding of work can be as rare as it
is transformative. What is a doctrinal view of work? How does God view
work and the work of His children? How does a right understanding of work
within God's creation order effect our experience, attitude, and approach to
our own work?

Most of us, as Christian businessmen and women, have carried with us no more than a vague and general awareness of the role of work in God's plan, and of His expectations for our work. But what is the actual origin and purpose of work as designed by God? For many of us the scripture that we most associate with that question comes at the expulsion of Adam and Eve from the garden,

> Cursed is the ground because of you;
> In toil you will eat of it
> All the days of your life.
> Both thorns and thistles it shall grow for you;
> And you will eat the plants of the field;
> By the sweat of your face
> You will eat bread,
> Till you return to the ground,
> Because from it you were taken;
> For you are dust,
> And to dust you shall return.[17]

When we think of work we think of The Curse, the Lord's pronouncement of eviction as He removed Adam and Eve from the garden. Mistakenly, many of us view that moment as the effective beginning of the concept of and mandate for work. We think of the lives of Adam and Eve in the Garden up until that point as an exercise in outdoor power-lounging.

In truth when Adam and Eve left the Garden, work was not a new concept to them. In fact, the origination of work occurs much earlier, in the Garden. The scripture says at the introduction of Adam into the garden, "Then the LORD God took the man and put him into the Garden of Eden to cultivate it and keep it."[18] It is clear from this passage that work (cultivation and care)

---

[17] Gen 3:17-19
[18] Gen 2:15

was the purpose of Adam in the Garden. It is the very reason scripture gives us for God's placing of Adam in His Garden, "to cultivate and keep it."

This 'original work', the work of Adam in the Garden before the fall is worth deliberate consideration. Adam's responsibilities to 'cultivate and keep' provide us with the ideal model of human work.

Perhaps it should have come as no surprise to either of us when we discovered that one of the fundamental goals and objectives of Brian Buffini's company is "Filling and Keeping". Expressly, Buffini and Company strives each year to 'fill its events' and 'keep its clients'. Walking through Buffini and Company headquarters a visitor who stops any employ and asks about the company's goals and objectives will be assured of hearing, "Filling and Keeping." The simplicity of the Buffini and Company's goal nearly cloaks its profundity. The objective of all of Buffini and Company's employees: "Filling and Keeping" remarkably parallels the original objective of work given by God to Adam. In defining the objective of its employees' efforts in a way that corresponds wonderfully to the original objective which was given to humanity for work, Buffini and Company has allowed its employs and it leadership to pursue their work according to its original design. The results have been extraordinary.

In the Garden, Adam enjoyed perfect fellowship with His Creator and perfect harmony within the creation order. We can assume that he did not toil nor sweat. All God had given him dominion over cooperated and submitted to his efforts. Interestingly Adam's work in the garden was not done for his own provision. It was not done in order that he could feed himself and Eve. God was providing for the every need of Adam. Adam's responsibility was to cultivate and keep that of the Lord's which had been entrusted to him. Adam worked the Garden simply to fulfill the purpose that God had placed him in the Garden to fulfill. Adam's work was all and only about purpose.

Adam's purpose becomes the benchmark for the work of all humanity. In the Hebrew, the word 'cultivate' is translated from the word *'abod'*. Abod can also more literally be translated: to serve. The word 'keep' is translated from the word *'shamar'*. Shamar means to keep or to protect. Adam's purpose in the Garden was to 'abod' and 'shamar'. That simple charge provides what is in essence humanity's first job description, "to serve and protect."

It is clear then that work was created and ordained by God for man, prior to and independent of the Curse. Work was in fact an integral part of the Creation order and the perfect relationship that man shared with the Creator and all of His creation. Work was the divinely appointed duty and responsibility of man in the Garden. In that light we can begin to see the intrinsic dignity, honor, and blessing of work as it was ordained by God. What wonderful work Adam's work in the Garden must have been!

Because he enjoyed perfect fellowship with God, Adam also enjoyed perfect peace and security. The Garden cooperated fully with Adam's efforts. His work was free from "toil" and "the sweat" of his face. He enjoyed the surpassing rest of God and in that rest he did the work that God had appointed to him.

Because for all of our lives we have lived and worked under the Curse, in our minds the ideas of work and rest are diametrically opposed. Work of any kind that does not include toil, sweat, and strife is spectacularly foreign to us. To our minds, toil, sweat, and strife are the very attributes that qualify an activity as work. After all, as the saying goes, "No pain, no gain." But pain was not God's original intention in the creation of work. Nor was toil or sweat.

Think about it, Adam was the gardener in a Garden that he did not need to weed or water. He worked in the Garden before there were, "thorns and thistles." He was gardener in a Garden designed by God to be automatically irrigated.[19] In today's day and age that is like a CEO who doesn't go to

---

[19] Genesis 2:10

meetings or talk on the telephone. The perfection of God's creation and Adam's place in it allowed him to complete his work without labor, toil or sweat. Because Adam enjoyed unbroken fellowship with God, his work was marked with all of the immeasurable delight of God's presence. His perfect relationship with the Father meant that he wanted for nothing; his work was not for gain or for profit. He did not even tend the Garden for his own provision; God provided for his every need. Instead, Adam's work was for one purpose only, the Glory of God.

This is the blueprint for the work of humanity. This is the quality, character, and motivation ordained by God in the very invention of work. God created work, he gave it to man, that it would be a blessing. In his work Adam was given a place and a context for the expression of his transcendent purpose, to glorify God. In his wisdom and compassion God gave man an active role in the tending of his marvelous creation and the unfolding of his perfect plan.

So we can conclude then that Adam's work in the Garden, the original work of man and the divine design of work itself is all about the transcendent purpose of glorifying God. It had nothing to do with increased wealth, status, or security. It had nothing to do with provision. It did not include toil, sweat, or even labor. Instead it was marked by a profound rest, the perfect rest found in unbroken fellowship with God Almighty.

If we are able to reconcile the two seemingly opposing ideas of work and rest, we are better able to understand the work as it was originally ordained and carried out by Adam. What does it mean to experience rest while engaged in work?

Matt grew up in the San Diego area. His father is an avid golfer whose home course for years was a public municipal course called Torrey Pines. Matt's father's passion for golf fascinated both he and his younger brother. For years and years, every Thursday morning at 4 a.m. the boys would hear the old man's Honda fire to life and back out of the garage as their dad headed out into the morning darkness for his weekly game.

Because it is the nature of fathers and sons, the boys were captivated by this game that their dad talked about often. They were intrigued by the pursuit that got him out of bed and into the Honda at 4 am each Thursday. Their attention was held rapt by this sport that led their dad to essentially declare "all family holidays" on the 4 Sundays a year that the PGA Majors finish.

In the summers, beginning when Matt was about 10 years old, his dad would sometimes let one of his 2 young sons come along as his caddie. To be invited to come along into this nearly sacred environment was a revelation. Summer is generally a time for young boys to sleep in, but the waking nudge from his dad at 3:30 am initiated a jolt of excitement rather than a sleepy groan. Matt would rocket out of bed, pull on the pants and shirt he had laid out, smash his feet into his shoes, and climb into his dad's car. The drive down the highway through the dawn darkness and patches of coastal fog was magical. Arriving in the still dark parking lot Matt would pull his dad's bag out of the old hatchback while his dad sat on the bumper to pull on his golf shoes. In the early quiet the "scrape-click-crunch" sound made by the metal spikes of others golfers in the parking lot, traveled out through the fog to the father and son.

After putting the bag in the line to the starter's booth, they would meet up with his dad's playing buddies in the coffee shop behind the 18th green. Matt would get an English muffin and listen to the men tell stories and talk about the articles in the newspapers as they waited for the light of dawn. At the first crack the groups would be sent off and the round would begin with Matt carrying the bag, oversized for his scrawny frame, down the first fairway alongside his father. His dad included him in each shot selection, just like a real caddie, and in the commentary running in his mind. The bag was heavy and 18 holes is more than 4 miles long, but Matt never complained. In fact he would have quickly volunteered to carry the bag another 18 holes.

Outside of fishing with his dad, caddying for him was one of the most magical and looked forward to experiences of Matt's childhood. Every bit of the process, from waking up at 3:30 am to sitting back in the coffee shop after the round was exciting and enjoyable. Why? To Matt, caddying for his dad meant being with his dad. It meant walking with him. It meant being invited into his life and his favorite pursuit. The 3:30 am wake up call, 4 mile hike, 30 pound bag, and dew soggy shoes were all part of the untainted joy for the young boy. The better the job he did, the prouder his dad became, and the more Matt enjoyed the experience.

A few years later in High School, Matt worked briefly as a caddie at a local private golf club. Waking up at 5 am was a brutal exercise. He hated it. The drive to the course in his old VW was a monotonous trudge filled with thoughts of quitting. Once at the course Matt was forced to quickly begin posturing against other caddies to get a 'loop'. If he did get out on the course, the bags he carried seemed to be filled with lead. The rounds were interminably long. The sun beat down on the top of his head. The shoulder straps cut into his skin and the golfers seemed cold and distant. The entire relationship that Matt tried to forge over those 18 holes was designed to create enough appreciation or sympathy to warrant a tip.

It is clear that in a short matter of years Matt had two radically different experiences doing the same work. For the first work, he carried a bag half as big as his body and was paid in English muffins and cokes. He loved that work and would have carried that bag until he dropped so long as it was for his father. For the second work, he had grown into the bag and was paid a fair wage. But he despised the work and the people he did it for. It was toil and sweat to make a living on a golf course which his father never played.

The allegory is obvious and simple enough. As a 10 year old, Matt experienced remarkable rest while engaged in what was clearly work. That rest had its origin in the delight which sprung from his simple purpose, service to and fellowship with his father. Likewise, Adam's rest was not a result of working before the Curse (and the toil and sweat that would accompany work thereafter), but rather from the perfect fulfillment of his purpose, serving and fellowshipping with His Heavenly Father.

Understanding the origin, design, and purpose for work, we are also able to develop a right understanding of the effect of the Curse upon work. We see that work was not something that God Cursed man with. Work is a blessing given by God to man. In His sovereign wisdom and grace God did not require man to forfeit the gift of work as he left the Garden. Instead, like all aspects of human life work was to be carried out under the Curse and within the radically different context that was created at the Fall of Man.

The Reality of Work

An understanding of the origin and ultimate purpose of work as ordained and displayed in the Garden can have a profound impact on every Christian's daily work. The reality however, is that work under the curse is still characterized, as the Lord commanded that it would be, by "toil", "sweat", "thorns and thistles." Work under the Curse remains a scratching of the earth in an effort to provide for our families.

The landscape of our work, our literal workplaces, has changed from perfectly cooperative, to perfectly un-cooperative. No doubt Murphy's Law sprang from the reality of life and work under the curse, "If something can go wrong, it will." The mechanics of work were dramatically altered upon man's eviction from the Garden. Competition, interpersonal conflict, deceit, greed, laziness, pride, and failure were all introduced as obstacles and realities within the workplace. The brothers Cain and Abel, who we can view as the first businessmen outside the Garden, provide us with a clear preview of what work would look like from that point forward. Cain was a farmer and Abel was a rancher. The events that sprang out of the context of their work provide a remarkable contrast to their father Adam's work in the Garden,

> "Abel was a keeper of flocks, but Cain was a tiller of the ground. So it came about in the course of time that Cain brought an offering to the LORD of the fruit of the ground. Abel, on his part also brought of the firstlings of his flock and of their fat portions. And the LORD had regard for Abel and for his offering; but for Cain and for his offering He had no regard. So Cain became very angry and his countenance fell. Then the LORD said to Cain, "Why are you angry? And why has your countenance fallen? If you do well, will not your countenance be lifted up? And if you do not do well, sin is crouching at the door; and its desire is for you, but you must master it." Cain told Abel his brother. And it came about when they were in the field, that Cain rose up against Abel his brother and killed him." Gen 4:2-8

In light of the reality illustrated in the story of Cain and Abel and the everyday of our work experience, what is the purpose of work after the Curse? Certainly we understand that the curse remains in effect and that all of our work this side of the Lord's return is done under the curse. The certainty of its influence and effects is as foundational as any of God's pronouncements. It cannot be thwarted, countered, neutralized, or avoided. So long as the Lord tarries in His return our workplaces will be uncooperative and our work will be marked by "toil" and "sweat". Do the inevitable "thorns and thistles" -competition, interpersonal conflict, deceit, greed, laziness, pride, and failure change the purpose of work? Does the blessing of work remain?

The great and central kicker of man's fall and the eviction from the Garden is the alienation it produced, the breaking of the perfect fellowship that man had enjoyed with our Heavenly Father. It was fellowship with God that man was designed for. It was fellowship with the Father that provided the perfect rest of Adam. It was fellowship with God that gave rise to the purpose of Adam and Adam's work.

In man's alienation from God there is the attendant disruption in that perfect rest and in man's ability to pursue the purpose for his work. Apart from God, man is no longer able to experience rest in his work. Estranged from God man is no longer able to pursue the divine purpose of his work. Man's purpose apart from God became finite and individual. He scratches the earth, toils and sweats to provide for his wants. The transcendent purpose of service and fellowship with the Father is, along with paradise, lost.

This is the very state, the state of Cain, that the majority of businesses today find themselves. Their purpose is common and finite, more profits. They're activity is marked with rush and anxiety and not the rest of God. They are businesses which exist and are run by individuals who remain unreconciled to God. Absent the fellowship of the author of all work, they're labor lacks all transcendent purpose. Work apart from the Lord, work that lacks purpose is a chasing after wind. This is the character of the work that King Solomon, the wisest man to ever live and presumed writer of Ecclesiastes, lamented:

> "Utterly meaningless! Everything is meaningless.
> What does man gain from all his labor at which he toils under the sun?"[20]

Alienation from God shatters purpose. There is no amount of profits (Solomon was the world's richest man), there exists neither title nor conquest; there is no esteem of an industry which can provide meaning apart from God. Work was designed, created, ordained, and finally given as a gift to man by God. It can not have purpose apart from Him. Alienated from God, the transcendent purpose of work evaporates.

---

[20] Ecclesiastes 1:2-3

The Restoration of Purpose

In and out of work, estrangement and alienation from God is the singular human problem. To the glory of God, the Gospel of Jesus Christ - His perfect life, suffering, death, resurrection, and ascension, is the Good News plainly because of the reconciliation and restoration that it provides. The Gospel of Christ Jesus then has a profound impact on work. As the pastor and writer Kent Hughes puts it, "To be sure, God does not remove the curse and its painful, sweaty toil, but He does replace the meaninglessness."[21]

Jesus Christ restores the Christian to fellowship with God the Father and in doing so restores him/her to the transcendent purpose of work. The toil and sweat present outside the Garden remain, but the original purpose is returned. So it is that we may now truly understand the command of scripture when it says, "Whatever you do, work at it with all your heart, as working for the Lord, not for men,...It is the Lord Christ you are serving."[22] Returned also is the rest available in the Lord and in the midst of toil and sweat we may understand the Word of the Lord when He declares, "For my yoke is easy and my burden is light."[23]

Though we live, breath, and work outside the gates of the Garden, the remarkable intimacy and personal fellowship with God which Adam enjoyed in his daily work, is the same intimacy and personal fellowship that Jesus Christ has ushered us into. We are restored also to the simple transcendent purpose for our daily work - to serve God and protect that which He has given to us.

---

[21] *Disciples of a Godly Man*, R. Kent Hughes,

[22] Colossians 3:23-24

[23] Matthew 11:30

> *The king's heart is like channels of water in the hand of the*
> *LORD;*
> *He turns it wherever He wishes. - Proverbs 21:1*

In the previous chapter we explored the origin of work and its ultimate purpose as designed and ordained by God. It is clear that there exists in all vocations and at all levels of work a commonality of Godly purpose. Under the eyes of God, the dignity of a hospital orderly's work is none less than that of a Fortune 500 CEO. Most importantly, the ability of the Christian worker to pursue God's ordained purpose within their work is no less from one honest vocation to the next. God's purpose is equally active in the most menial of work as it is in the most prestigious.

In the same way, we can appropriately apply the Bible's teaching on work to all types and levels of work. God's view of work is, in essence, universally applicable and clearly laid out for His people to discover. Biblical wisdom regarding work is readily available: the word "work" appears 391 times in each the NASB and NIV translations. As we considered in the previous chapter, the Lord provides us with clear and direct guidance as to the attitude and character that we as Christians are to bring to work. These scriptural references deal with the full spectrum of work that God's beloved are engaged in. A right understanding of the origin and purpose of work is as essential and edifying to the carpet installer as it is to the carpet company owner.

But does God have specific instruction, expectations, and insight for business owners and leaders? There were no CEO's, corporations, Boards of Directors, vice-presidents, or annual reports in Biblical times; but is there insight and information in the Bible that is specific to corporate governance and business leadership? In the Bible, can we discover instruction, insight and wisdom regarding business leadership that is in addition to the Lord's teaching on work in general? If so, is it possible that as a community, we have by and large missed some of the information available to us? In this chapter we will seek out and explore Biblical realities and truths which can be specifically applied to the role of business owner and leader today.

The Veil of Familiarity

The Bible is the story of God and His creation, the unfolding of His plan, and the revelation of His Glory. The finiteness, struggle, and ordinary nature of our work can make our jobs very difficult to reconcile with our experience of an infinite, perfect, and extraordinary God. In infinity past He existed majestic and powerful; He spoke our world into existence; He orders and ordains each breeze, each war, each peace, each breath, each wave, each birth, each word, and each death. He has built nations, raised up and toppled all Kings and Rulers, Himself become flesh and blood, and orchestrated the salvation of His church. Is it any wonder that when we consider the majestic works of His hand, our work which is done at our ordinary desk, in our regular company, with our everyday employees can seem outside of wondrous story of God?

It is possible that the familiarity of our work has had a dimming effect on our labor. Familiarity turns the extraordinary to ordinary and can rob us of wonder. Many babies are enchanted by a miraculous wheel of tumbling paddles, racing one after the other in an endless chase that spins in orbit above their heads. At a certain age their attention can be held rapt for hours by this wonderful and giant mobile. It is an extraordinary contraption, but as the days go by the marvel of it begins to fade and the extraordinary becomes ordinary to the growing child. As soon as their language develops the child is able to label the once marvelous contraption, and with that labeling the "ceiling fan" loses the last of its wonder.

As humans we have a remarkable and damning ability to let the veil of familiarity blind us to even the most wonderful and miraculous. The nation of Israel was guided in the wilderness by a pillar of cloud by day and a pillar of fire by night. It was an obvious, miraculous, and comforting sign to the people - I am with you. Additionally the Lord demonstrated His presence, protection, and provision for Israel in miracle after miracle. Still it took only time to breed the familiarity which blinded the people to the obvious and present signs of God's leading and protection - the pillar of cloud and fire, the parting of the Red Sea, the destruction of the Egyptian Army, Manna every morning. Soon the people began to grumble and fret. What will we drink? What will we eat? Where are we going? Are we safe? God's pillar remained before them, manna appeared each morning, and still the kindness of God had somehow become ordinary to the people and Israel took it for granted.

Our jobs and companies have the same feel of the everyday, the ordinary, and the supremely secular. The familiar everyday and ordinary quality of our work and our companies has somehow dislocated that work from the reality of our faith and our origin. The familiarity of it, in a way the concrete reality of our experience with work has removed it from the context of the abiding eternal reality of God's purposes. Evidence of that prevailing dynamic is familiar to most Christian business leaders: We constantly long to infuse what we see as the secular (our work) with the sacred (our faith). We ask the question, "How do I pursue my Christian walk in the secular business world?" and we grow frustrated by the priorities of the corporate world. Consider how that prevailing frustration might be turned on its head in light of the realization that no matter how ordinary or familiar, the work of the Christian is by virtue of its origin and purpose, sacred and NOT secular.

Adding to the illusion that our modern work is dislocated from God's design or intimate presence is the context within which we work; the very look and feel of our companies and the work they do. Technology, transportation, and communication have had a profound effect on the look and feel of modern culture, and as a result an even more profound effect on our experience of work. The stage that the Lord has ordained these current generations to live their lives upon has a radically different setting than the stories of the Bible. We do not live in tents and most of us do not work with our hands. Modern "progress" has fashioned a powerful illusion which tempts each of us to believe that we do not wait upon the mercy of God for our daily provision.

Consider how we take even the most basic necessities of life, like water, for granted. Throughout human history the search for and availability of water has determined the location, prosperity, and destruction of cities and civilizations. Both of us live in San Diego which has renowned weather in part due to its remarkably arid climate. Yet in an area which is essentially a desert, millions of people live and work. Water springs forth at every turn, from the walls of our homes, from pop-up spigots in the grass and on hillsides, from silver boxes in parks and at least one designated "water closet" in every building. In the same way, in our country food is a given, travel is a common convenience, and scientific medicine offers our culture's most enticing hope.

And yet even though we drive BMW's and not camels, communicate across the globe via the Internet rather than hand delivered letters, and live in weather impervious homes rather than tents and mud huts, still we live our lives under the eyes of God. What if the facade of the familiar and the modern were burned away? What if we were given fresh eyes, the eyes of children, to see the plan and purposes of God in our lives as clearly as we see them in the figures of the Bible? Would we not be humbled to the point of awe at the reality that our every breath and heartbeat, let alone the whole of our existence and provision, is within the perfect intimate control of God Almighty? Would we see the purpose, blessing expectation and character of our work any differently than that of Adam's, Abel's, or Paul's? Will we not be judged before the same White Throne? Do we not depend upon the mercy of the same God? Are we not in equal need of the same perfect Savior? God is "the same yesterday and today and forever."[24] He does not have a sliding scale for us today, but is steadfast and faithful to the, "unchangeableness of His purpose."[25]

What if the language, titles, trappings, technologies, geographies, and culture of your position as a business owner and leader were burned away to reveal the eternal reality of your work? What would that reality reveal? What is the eternal and authentic position of the modern Christian business leader under the eyes of God?

Kings in Suits

In the western world the idea of true royalty is an utterly foreign concept. To talk of kings and kingdoms harkens back to an era long past. The idea of a king is at once alluring and antiquated. There is no human title so infused with power, authority, and majesty. And there is no title within the civilized world which has grown more unused or outdated. To imagine a good King is to imagine everything that the human heart longs for in a leader - goodness, authority, strength, power, wisdom, courage, and nobility. There is a part of every young boy which desires to be led into battle by a good King. There is a part of every young girl which wishes to be rescued by such a King.

The Bible is filled with kings. Its message is a proclamation of the King of Kings, Jesus Christ. Kingship is the major office which the Lord chooses to

---

[24] Hebrews 13:8

[25] Hebrews 6:17

use in the unfolding of His plan and His story. Kings, and the hearts of those kings play a momentous role in the progression of biblical history. The kings of Israel were created by God to be Theocratic agents by whom God would rule over and bless His people. In observing God's relationship with the king's of the Bible we are provided with powerful insight into the character of God. Likewise we are provided with a clear picture of the character qualities that God both loves and hates in the leaders He raises up. Kings, the wrestlings of their hearts, their obedience to God, their triumphs, their foolishnesses, their pride, their prayers, and their passions play an extraordinary role in the divine narrative that is the Lord's unfolding plan. Adam, Abraham, Melchizedek, Pharoah, Saul, David, Solomon, Jehoshaphat, Hezekiah, and Herod, (to name only a few of the Biblical Kings) were all kings in office if not specifically in title. The story of these rulers and leaders is the story of their hearts, their obedience or defiance of the Lord, and the direct effect that their hearts and actions had upon the fate of their people. It is the people, specifically the people of God, who are the subjects of the story of God.

Chronologically the Biblical account of God's people ended about 100 years after the resurrection of Jesus Christ. To be certain, the written revelation of God's Holy Word, the Bible, is complete and finished; however, the story of God and His people continues beyond the inspired chronicle given to us in the Bible. The Lord continues to unfold His perfect story. His plan of salvation endures. His intimacy and nearness does not abate and His coming only draws nearer. If we are certain of the continuation of the story and plan of God, we should also consider the role of king in that plan. As prominent and integral a part as God has, in His wisdom, given kings to play within the Bible, we must ask the question: What has become of the role of King today?

In chapter 1 we briefly discussed the prominence of Corporations in modern life and we examined the pervasive impact and effect that Corporations have on the daily lives of people. In this current age companies and corporations deeply impact and effect the lives of employees and customers to a degree that far outstrips the impact and effect of government. Today's companies and corporation are the worldly kingdoms of modern day. They are the agents of provision and security for their employees and those employee families; they're territory and land is called market share; they method of conquest is called merger or business warfare instead of siege or pillage; the largest are known and have influence in far away lands; their creeds are called core values; their decrees are called memos; their crests are called logos; and their Kings are called CEOs.

The implication of our discussion is clear; in ways more real than allegorical, the CEOs and business owners of today are the equivalent of the kings of the biblical age. Even the language and titles have changed very little. If you are your company's owner or leader you are more than likely its Chief Executive Officer. You are the Chief and a Chief is, "One who is highest in rank or authority; a leader."[26] Chief is, in truth, just another word for King. In fact, many biblical references to minor kings may be more appropriately translated as 'chief' to denote their more local dominion. This excerpt is from the entry for "King" in the McClintock and Strong Biblical Encyclopedia:

> "Many persons are called " kings" in Scripture whom we should rather denominate chiefs or leaders; and many single towns, or towns with their adjacent villages, are said to have kings. Hence we need not be surprised at seeing that so small a country as Canaan contained thirty-one kings who were conquered (Josh 12:9,24), besides many who no doubt escaped the arms of Joshua. Adonibezek himself, no very powerful king, mentions seventy kings whom he had subdued and mutilated (Judg 1:7; 1 Kings 4:21; 20:1,16)."[27]

---

[26] American Heritage Dictionary, Fourth Edition

[27] McClintock and Strong Encyclopedia

Perhaps you are also the "Chairman of the Board". If so, you are titled "Chairman" because you occupy the "Chair" of authority. You are the man (or woman) who is in The Chair. What chair is that? In its original meaning it is the Chair of Authority (the degree of authority dependent upon your Corporate ByLaws, the equivalent to the laws of a kingdom). Literally it is the seat of power. In biblical days that 'seat of power' was called the Throne. The only one who could sit on it was called the King. If you are the Chairman you are sitting in the Chair of Authority; If you are sitting in the Chair of Authority you are sitting on the Throne; If you are sitting on the Throne, you are the King.

Consider again the blinding veil of familiarity and its effect on how we hear and wear those corporate titles. In a nation which nurses a 200 year old hangover grudge against the monarchy of England, we are nevertheless a nation filled with CEOs and Chairmen - Chiefs and Throne sitters - a land of many Kings. No matter if you lead a company of 5 or 5,000 as your company's leader, you are a King in suit.

King of Kings

If we see the landscape of companies as kingdoms - some large and some small - led by so many kings, then what insight, truth, and instruction does the Bible offer to the today's corporate King? If we consider not just the origin and purpose of work in general, but that sacred work within the unique and special context of a King and Leader's position, what wisdom can we seek from God's word?

We have identified 4 broad principles that God clearly reveals in His word in regards to Kings and their Kingdoms. The pervasiveness of kings in the bible means that there are many more principles, much greater wisdom, and countless more examples which we are not able to address here. Indeed, understanding your leadership role within the context of King makes each

Biblical story which includes a King rich in the specific wisdom and insight it offers to leaders.

It is important for us to be clear that there is a clear distinction between the general, earthly office of King and the Hebrew Monarchy. The Throne of David is now and forever occupied by the King Jesus. So as we discuss modern day kings we do so in the earthly sense and not in regards to the Hebrew Monarchy.

The entire Bible, of course, points to this one true and final King - King Jesus who is the King of Kings. The one who rules and reigns upon the eternal throne. Most of us have heard the title King of Kings often enough that it has become simply another of the Lord's superlative titles, denoting his supremacy above all. But consider what King of Kings means at its most basic level. Jesus Christ is the sovereign of the earthly sovereigns; He is the ruler and authority of the earthy Kings. They are under His dominion, power and control.

Even those Kings, those CEOs, which deny Christ remain under His authority. His Kingly dominion is complete and absolute,

> Heaven is My throne and the earth is My footstool.
> Where then is a house you could build for Me?
> And where is a place that I may rest?
> 2 "For My hand made all these things,
> Thus all these things came into being," declares the LORD.[28]

By the Grace of God we have been made subjects of His kingdom and children of the King. We do not deny Christ the King but joyfully submit to Him and His authority. If you are a business leader, a modern day King, then these 4 principles from the Bible should provide you with valuable insight.

---

[28] Isa 66:1-2

1. **It is not your kingdom**

   Your business, like your life, is not your own. All of it is God's.

   "For every beast of the forest is Mine,
   The cattle on a thousand hills.
   I know every bird of the mountains,
   And everything that moves in the field is Mine.
   If I were hungry I would not tell you,
   For the world is Mine, and all it contains."[29]

   He has entrusted it to you to "rule" over according to His word, His purposes, and His will. Your stewardship is not primarily focused on the company's assets but upon its people. You are placed not over a balance sheet but over a community.

2. **God raised you to authority**

   Regardless of how you have experienced your career, it is not your hard work, intelligence, courage or even piety which has elevated you to your current position. The sovereign will of God alone has raised you to your position and His will alone will sustain you there. God both raises up and removes leaders, "After He had removed him (Saul), He raised up David to be their king."[30]

   As the leader of your business and its effective King, you have been given authority over the kingdom that is comprised in the totality of your company. You determine the direction of the company, its pace, its brand, its values, its culture, and ultimately its purpose. God has raised you up to your position that you may do exactly that.

   ---

   [29] Ps 50:10-12
   [30] Acts 13:22

For better or for worse, you are precisely the person whom God in His infinite wisdom has ordained as steward over His company. He has raised you up for His good purposes. Throughout the Bible God raised up good kings, wicked kings, good kings who became wicked, and wicked kings who became good. The kings were the agent of both blessing and rebuke to the kingdoms they ruled over. God is working in the lives which your company impacts (employees, customers, vendors) in part through His placing you in a leadership position.

3.   **Your heart means everything.**

The condition of your heart is the defining factor in the impact, health, direction, success, and legacy of your company.   As your company's leader you do determine the direction of the company, its pace, its brand, its values, its culture, and ultimately its purpose; but what is the origin of that direction, pace, brand, value set, and purpose in you?   In the end it's all about your heart.   That is the reason for the title of this book, *The Heart of Business*.

> The good man out of the good treasure of his heart brings forth what is good; and the evil man out of the evil treasure brings forth what is evil; for his mouth speaks from that which fills his heart. [31]

The greatest earthly King the world has ever known was King David. Above all else, David is known even to this very day by a singular character attribute - He was man after God's own heart. Your heart is the heart of your business and the heart is all that concerns the Lord.

---

[31] Luke 6:45

God sees not as man sees, for man looks at the outward appearance, but the LORD looks at the heart.[32]

4.   **God is directing your heart.**
We know that God hardens and softens the hearts of men according to His good purposes. For the Kings of the world, the Bible is even more explicit as to the complete control that God has over the heart of the leader,

> The king's heart is like channels of water
> in the hand of the LORD;
> He turns it wherever He wishes.[33]

In His sovereignty and wisdom God is leading and guiding you, directing the very heart that directs His company - yours.

We see then that the heart of a business is found within the breast of the businesses leader and that heart is controlled and directed by God. You business will rise and fall, your leadership will be blessed or frustrated, lives will be impacted, and a legacy will be developed not according to your intelligence, education, charisma, or determination, but according to the character, condition, will and purposes which God has placed within your heart - the heart of a king.

---

[32] 1 Sam 16:7-8
[33] Proverbs 21:1

As in water face reflects face,
So the heart of man reflects man. - Prov 27:19

The Heart

The human heart begins to beat for the first time 21 days after conception. Set into motion by a divine touch, the first beat is the genesis of a simple, repeating cycle known as the "heartbeat". That audible 'beat' of the heart is the primary sustainer and paramount evidence of any and all human life. The rhythm marked out by the pulse will continue for exactly the entire human lifetime (an average of 2.5 billion beats), drumming out a unique cadence within which all of that life will be conducted. Where there is the beat of a heart, there is life. So too when that rhythm ends, the life is over.

Both because of the human heart's necessity to physiological life and its proximity to the middle of the body, the heart has always been a universal symbol for center and for origin. Indeed, in our search for clarity we seek out the "heart of the matter", hoping to discover the core of an issue. The geographic and cultural center of a metropolis is the "heart of the city". And the player who embodies the spirit and persona of a team is often identified as the "heart of the team".

The Heart also implies truth. For better or for worse, important moments and words are said to "reveal our hearts". When a story, play, or movie captures the essence of life's tenderness we say it "has heart". A practiced listener may ask you to "share your heart" and in doing so be asking you to reveal your most honest feelings in regard to a personal issue.

The medical field, which has entire schools and hospitals dedicated to the science of the heart, uses the term 'cardiac' to denote all things related to that most important central human pump. Cardiac comes from the ancient Greek word for heart - 'kardia'. Kardia is defined as, "the center and seat of spiritual life, the soul or mind, as it is the fountain and seat of the thoughts, passions, desires, appetites, affections, purposes, endeavors." In Hebrew, the language of the Old Testament, the word for heart is 'leb', which interestingly is also the word for "mind".

Indeed the centrality, influence, and importance of the heart as understood by the Old Testament Jews and the early Christians is significantly broader than our understanding of the 'heart' today. Practical understanding of the 'heart' in our culture is confined to the physiological role of the organ within our circulatory systems. Use of the word 'heart' outside of its physical role is done strictly in an allegorical sense. It is merely an expression, such as the ones used at the beginning of the chapter. Because the scope of the biblical meaning and connotation of heart is so much broader than our present usage, it does us well to attempt to recapture a biblical understanding of the word 'heart' and confront the reality of its meaning and use in the scriptures.

The Heart of the Bible

In the Bible 'heart' certainly is the primary organ and physiological center of life. But it is also the seat of the inner man. The Hebrew mind and language did not separate body and soul in the way that we do: "The Hebrew contrasts two other concepts which are not found in the Greek and Latin tradition: "the inner self" and "the outer appearance" or, as viewed in a different context, "what one is to oneself" as opposed to "what one appears to be to one's observers.'"[34] The heart is the seat of the inner self, or as the author Brennan Manning might put it, "the authentic self."

In God's Word, 'heart' is also the seat of a person's very will. The inclinations and desires of man spring from the heart. In Exodus we see the decree, "whoever is of a willing heart, let him bring it as the LORD'S contribution."[35] Clearly the heart is seen as the agent of willing. Today we are apt to ascribe decisions of will, especially in business, to the mind. We intellectually precede though a logically and rationally ordered process of consideration to arrive at our decisions.

Certainly such intellectual, prayerful consideration should in fact occur; prudence and diligence are godly characteristics. But to endeavor to remove desires and inclinations from business decisions of leadership by attempting to remove them from the heart and make them with the 'mind', is to attempt to separate that which God views as one and the same. Indeed, 'heart' is additionally understood in the bible as the seat of knowledge and wisdom. In other words, heart is understood as the location and origin of what we understand as 'mind'. Proverbs 23:7 clearly describes the heart as the origin and location of thought, "For as he thinks in his heart, so is he."

Nearly all of what we would describe as mental processes are, in the Bible, heart processes. Time after time, knowledge and 'knowing' take place 'in the heart' and are ascribed to the heart, "Thus you are to <u>know in your heart</u> that the LORD your God was disciplining you just as a man disciplines his son." [36] Consideration and imagination are born in the heart, "Then you will <u>say in your heart</u>, 'Who has begotten these for me,'"[37] Memorization too is

---

[34] Vine's Expository Dictionary of Old Testament Words

[35] Ex 35:5

[36] Deut 8:5

[37] Isa 49:21

understood as taking place in the heart, "My son, do not forget my teaching, But let your heart keep my commandments."[38]

The heart is the seat of conscience and morality,

> "How does one respond to the revelation of God and of the world around him? Job answers: "...my heart shall not reproach me as long as I live" 27:6. On the contrary, "David's heart smote him..." 2 Sam 24:10. The "heart" is the fountain of man's deeds: "...in the integrity of my heart and innocency of my hands I have done this" Gen 20:5; cf. v. 6. David walked "in uprightness of heart" 1 Kings 3:6 and Hezekiah "with a perfect heart" Isa 38:3 before God. Only the man with "clean hands, and a pure heart" Ps 24:4 can stand in God's presence."[39]

The heart is, less surprisingly, also the seat of emotions. God commands, "Love the LORD your God with all your heart and with all your soul and with all your strength."[40]

Finally, the heart is clearly the point of rebellion and the seat of pride as well:

> "No, in your heart you work unrighteousness; On earth you weigh out the violence of your hands."[41]

> "the intent of man's heart is evil from his youth"[42]

---

[38] Prov 3:1

[39] Vine's Expository Dictionary of Old Testament Words

[40] Deut 6:5

[41] Ps 58:2

[42] Gen 8:21

Finally, this natural condition of man's heart, makes the heart the nexus point in the fruit of salvation. Indeed in God's plan of salvation sinful man's hardened heart, dead and hardened to the point of stone, is supernaturally replaced. Quite literally God's beloved are given a heart transplant, "Moreover, I will give you a new heart and put a new spirit within you; and I will remove the heart of stone from your flesh and give you a heart of flesh. I will put My Spirit within you and cause you to walk in My statutes, and you will be careful to observe My ordinances."[43]

So we can see then that the biblical view of the heart, God's view of the heart, is truly breathtaking in scope. The heart is the seat of physical life, will, desire, inclination, emotion, knowledge, wisdom, intellect, imagination, memory, conscience, morality, rebellion and pride. It is also the effected subject of salvation. In short, in God's view and economy, the heart is the center and wellspring of all life[44], be it physical, spiritual, intellectual, or emotional. The heart is the central reality of man. As an object is the defining reality determining the shape and character of the shadow it generates, so the heart is the defining reality determining the shape and character of the life it that it sustains. The condition and character of the heart determines the condition and character of the life.

The Heart's Effect

The heart's role within the physical being directly parallels its role within the spiritual being. A heart that is weak and failing with disease results in a weak and failing physical body. Atherosclerosis is one of the most common heart related diseases. *Sclerosis* is from the Greek meaning - hardness. Individuals who develop atherosclerosis have a hardening of their arteries caused by a build up of fatty deposits called plaque. In a literal and physical way, these individuals have developed heart systems that are hardened. This hardening

---

[43] Ezek 36:26-28

[44] Proverbs 4:23

is seriously debilitating and can result in heart attacks, stokes, and other life threatening events. Because the heart is the central organ of life, a weak or hardened heart dramatically effects the entire physical being. Energy fails, alertness flags, passion wanes, and other diseases and afflictions begin to creep in. Gangrene, pneumonia, atrophy, depression, among many others ailments are all associated with heart disease. As the physical heart grows sick, life begins to leave the body.

Contrastingly a healthy and vital heart produces a healthy and vital body. The healthy heart provides the body with the life and energy it requires to pursue the purposes of God and enjoy His creation to its fullest. An individual with a healthy heart can grow and stretch their body. A healthy heart pumps rich life giving and restoring blood in ample supply to every corner of the body. That blood carries nutrients, oxygen, and disease fighters to each cell, and whisks away waste and byproducts. That is why the individual with the healthy heart is best able to fight of disease and to heal quickly from injury.

Likewise, the spiritual and intellectual aspects of our being are equally shaped by the condition of our hearts. It is true that on the most basic spiritual level a 'hardened heart' leads to affliction and is associated with spiritual death in the same way that a physical 'hardened heart' leads to affliction and death. The wonderful account of Moses, Israel, and Pharaoh provides ample evidence:

> Then the LORD said to Moses, "Go to Pharaoh, for I have
> hardened his heart and the heart of his servants, that I may
> perform these signs of Mine among them, 2 and that you may tell
> in the hearing of your son, and of your grandson, how I made a
> mockery of the Egyptians and how I performed My signs among
> them, that you may know that I am the LORD."[45]

---

[45] Ex 10:1-2

Over and over the heart of Pharaoh is hardened and the Lord's signs bring affliction and plague upon Pharaoh's kingdom - Egypt. Against all reason and logic and in the face of the demonstrated evidence of God's presence and power, Pharaoh's hardened heart compels him to foolishness and sin. As the condition of Pharaoh's heart grows worse he eventually leads his army in pursuit of the fleeing Israelites and into complete annihilation under the waves of the Red Sea.

It is at this jumping off point that it is vitally important that we do no slip into an allegorical frame of thinking. In the Bible, the spiritual heart is as concrete a reality as the physical one. In fact, a compelling case can be made that its importance and reality far outstrips that of the physical heart. While we will have use for our physical heart in the short fleeting years of our life on this earth, it is our spiritual heart that is eternal. It is our spiritual heart that is seen by God. It is our spiritual heart that will be judged by Him.

The heart of David is a supreme contrast to the heart of Pharaoh. It is not hard to make the case that outside of His son Jesus Christ, the Father loved no man more than David. And the Lord makes it imminently clear that it was the heart of David which is so pleasing to Him. Indeed it is David's heart that provides his most famous title, "a man after God's own heart." When the prophet Samuel was searching for the Lord's anointed (to become King in the stead of Saul) he was led to the house of Jesse. As he was beginning to size up Eliab, one of Jesse's impressive sons (and an older brother of David), the Lord gave Samuel the wonderful instructions, "Do not look at his appearance or at the height of his stature, because I have rejected him; for God sees not as man sees, for man looks at the outward appearance, **but the LORD looks at the heart.**"[46] Through each of Jesse's sons the prophet Samuel went, until none were left except the youngest, David, who was in the field tending the sheep. Still just a young boy, Jesse and his older sons did not consider David to be

---

[46] 1 Sam 16:7-8

of a stature that warranted consideration. And yet it was this shepherd boy David who the Lord would give to do mighty things, and raise up to be the greatest of the earthly kings. It was through David that He would establish the line and throne of the coming King of Kings, Jesus Christ.

The inescapable truth is this: *As the heart goes, so goes all of life.* That foundational truth not only guides and impacts every personal human life, but it also profoundly impacts modern business and its leadership. Your heart does not simply effect your company; it profoundly defines it. The hardened heart of Pharaoh led his entire company of soldiers to destruction. The tender heart of David was used to establish the single line and Throne that would deliver a Savior into the world. The desire and disposition of your heart will impart to your company its values, set its course, shape its goals, determine it methodologies, inspire its culture, and define its success.

Heart Process Loop

The centrality of the heart within the being of each man, its ultimate importance under the eyes of God, and its dominion over the faculties of will, mind, body, and emotion ensure that the character and condition of a leader's heart has enormous impact on every facet of the business that they have been raise to lead. In an effort to represent the extraordinary and dynamic role that the heart of a Christian leader plays in a company's direction and success we developed the Heart Process Loop. Instructed by the scriptures, The Heart Process Loop is a simple representation of the inescapable cycle of origin, action and result that governs all business endeavors.

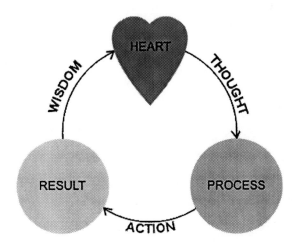

The **heart** of a leader is the seat of will, desire, inclination, emotion, knowledge, wisdom, intellect, imagination, memory, conscience, and morality. Originated, refined and extended outward from the desires and inclinations of that heart are **thoughts**.

These thoughts naturally lead to an activation of **process**. **Process** is the sequential progression (unique or standardized) of engagement which culminates in a decision. That decision is licensed and justified by the heart. That license and justification may come from:

> **Knowledge** - "Wingnuts have always sold well in the winter";

> **Wisdom** - "I am reluctant to hire a man who has been abused by his father."

> **Memory** - "I remember that woman from her speech last year. I'm going to say hello."

> **Desire** - "I want to make a difference in this young man's life. I'm going to mentor him."

Emotion - "I love this organization. They changed my life, now we can help them."

Imagination - "What if we…."

Morality - "It's the right thing to do."

The Decision Process gives rise to **actions**. **Actions** are the doings, sayings, and beings that are carried out within space and time. Most importantly, **actions are the outward expressions of the heart.** Such a view of our own actions and the actions of others can radically transform our lives.

> "The good man out of the good treasure of his heart brings forth what is good; and the evil man out of the evil treasure brings forth what is evil;"[47]

Necessarily all actions end in a **result**. A **result** is the consequence and sometimes ending of an action or operation. **Results**, according to the point of view, may be deemed positive or negative. The sovereignty of God assures us that every result is outside of our control.

Each **result**, both positive and negative, has the potential to give rise to **wisdom**. **Wisdom** is the ability to make the correct decision at the correct time. Wisdom is a gift from God which begins with the fear of God[48] and is cultivated and matured by reflection and knowledge of God's word. Honest assessment and prayerful reflection of any result, the actions which led to that result, the decision which initiated the actions, and the heart which gave rise to the decision against the knowledge of God and His word will increase wisdom. Because wisdom is seated within the heart, an increase in wisdom will produce a transformation of the heart.

---

[47] Luke 6:45
[48] Prov 1:7

Within this 'feedback' loop, you and your business change and evolve based upon the desires and motives of your heart. The results of your efforts, the fruit, as it were, repeatedly impact and instruct your heart. As your heart is reshaped by time and experience, it effects a change in your thoughts, which changes your process, which changes your actions, which again change your result. The process continues.

The Heart Process Loop describes a fundamentally true process of life. That truth holds for all hearts, those pure and those corrupt. It is true then that the desires of the corrupt heart will give rise to wrong process, which will produce dishonorable results. Likewise, from the pure heart will spring right desires, giving rise to correct process and honorable results.

For You do not delight in sacrifice, otherwise I would give it;
You are not pleased with burnt offering.
The sacrifices of God are a broken spirit;
A broken and a contrite heart, O God, You will not despise.
-Ps 51:16-17

We have defined and explored the impact and virtue of a transcendent
purpose. We have considered the nobility of the business leader. Most recently
we have begun an exploration of the centrality of the heart. At this point the
unfolding implications begin to develop a weighty feel. If your aim is to run
and grow a simple and humble business then to consider yourself as a 'king'
of sorts, and one literally raised to that position by the very hand of God
to do His purposes, is a daunting mantle. Furthermore the responsibility
of providing a purpose to your entire organization, in fact the inevitability
of providing that purpose - be it ordinary or transcendent, is a reality of
enormous significance. Finally, the understanding that it is your heart which
is the author of that purpose and which will consequently determine and
direct the impact, health, direction, success, and legacy of your business, can
be a nearly crushing awareness.

It is also an understanding which stands in near direct opposition to the commonly held view of successful business leadership. The world's view of modern leadership effectiveness and business success is built upon education, experience, intelligence, and personality. There is a pervasive, however unspoken, understanding that the 'heart' of the leader is actually of little or marginal importance, so long as that leader has the 'self made' qualities coupled with the natural gifts and abilities which make him/her an effective leader; all the while 'effectiveness' is measured simply by the maximization of profits. This entrenched view of modern organizational leadership vigorously resists and rejects the notion that something so intangible, uncontrollable, and immeasurable as the heart would be the determining factor in the direction and success of an organization. Why? Why would a distilled view of leadership, an ancient and a right view of leadership be so resisted?

Perhaps it is because, at its core, the world understands the futility that such an understanding appears to lead one to. After all, if it is the leader's heart that determines and directs the impact, health, direction, success, and legacy of an organization then there is a nearly perfect imperative to examine that heart. Examination of the heart is a stark exercise. If we turn to God's word to learn of our heart we find over and again a desperate picture. Our hearts begin bad "...the intent of man's heart is evil from his youth."[49] And they do not improve, "The heart is more deceitful than all else and is desperately sick."[50] Where then does that leave the leader who would lead with their heart?

Who of us can stand the honest examination of our hearts? Furthermore, who of us in good conscience would trust the character and purity of our own hearts as the determining agent of our business and the provision of its employees? None of us. Not when it is clear that our hearts are prone to wickedness from birth.

---

[49] Gen 8:21

[50] Jer 17:9

Instead, the natural man or woman in each of us would rather that our effort, perseverance, guile, intelligence, and experience be the determining factor. Most leaders are entrepreneurs in spirit and no matter what is required, we are prone to say, "let us strain and struggle, sweat and toil" to accomplish it.

We would rather that the outcome of our business be guided by a complex quotient of education, experience, intelligence, and personality that is of our own design. Let it be, in other words, upon the merits of our efforts that our businesses rise and fall. And if all of it must rest upon our shoulders then we are apt to say, "so be it" and all the more we believe that we are cultivating our own 'self-made' story. And so with our own efforts we paint a thousand shiny layers of lacquer upon the corrupt purposes of our heart. Indeed we plead, "Whatever the work required for success, let success be had according to that work."

What we cannot bear is to accept that the simple, inescapable and undisguisable character of our hearts is the determining factor in the quality and success of our leadership. For surely experience has taught each of us that the condition, disposition, and inclinations of our own hearts are strangely beyond our control. We know that there are no number of hours that we can put in, classes we can take, or methodologies we can employ which will change our hearts. While every fiber of us looks for the bootstraps by which we will pull ourselves and our organizations up to success, the 'heart-centric' view removes not only our bootstraps but our boots as well. We are exposed and left wanting.

It is a remarkable parallel to the condition of man. Oswald Chambers described so wonderfully the dynamic that persists in each one of us - the thorn of pride and the seemingly unquenchable drive for self sufficiency and self worth which it promotes.

"There is a certain pride in people that causes them to give and give, but to come and accept a gift is another thing. I will give my life to martyrdom; I will dedicate my life to service—I will do anything. But do not humiliate me to the level of the most hell-deserving sinner and tell me that all I have to do is accept the gift of salvation through Jesus Christ."[51]

We seem then to approach a type of spiritual conundrum. To confront the reality of a 'heart-centric' understanding of leadership is to also confront the devastating effects of sin and the certainty of the sickness of the heart. Is there any point to developing an understanding (however correct) of the centrality of a leader's heart within an organization if that heart is assuredly wicked? What good is the light of truth when it reveals depravity? Is not the gentle comfort which is bought with the illusion of self-determination, no matter how frail, preferable to the reality of an uncontrollable God's sovereignty in my life and my business?

Let's set these questions and thoughts aside for a moment and return to them at the chapter's end.

Losing Your Bootstraps

If a right understanding of the impact of the leader's heart prompts an unavoidable examination of the heart, it also should drive every Christian business leader to ask a single question: What type of heart does God desire?

We know that King David was a man after God's own heart, and that David's heart pleased God. But what type of heart did David possess? What is the character of a heart that is after God's? Clearly the scriptures tell us that

---

[51] *My Utmost for His Highest*, November 28, Oswald Chambers

God is looking for one that pleases Him, that His eyes are ranging over His creation seeking out the heart that is after His:

> The LORD has looked down from heaven
> upon the sons of men
> To see if there are any who understand,
> Who seek after God.[52]

And we must remember that God says His eyes do not see as our eyes see, "The LORD does not look at the things man looks at. Man looks at the outward appearance, but the LORD looks at the heart."[53] In a way, it seems that God is looking down upon creation with a divine type of x-ray vision, examining the hearts of men and women, searching for the heart that is pleasing to Him. Do we know what that heart looks like? Can we know? Can we know the type of heart that the Lord delights in? Is it quantifiable? Can it be articulated and defined? The answer, thankfully and wonderfully, is yes.

In His word, God clearly lays out for His people the heart that He desires and esteems; the heart that He is searching for.

> But to this one I will look, to him who is humble and contrite of
> spirit, and who trembles at My word."[54]

In the NIV translation it is put this way:

> This is the one I esteem:
> he who is humble and contrite in spirit,
> and trembles at my word.[55]

---

[52] Ps 14:2

[53] 1 Sam 16:7

[54] Isa 66:2

[55] Isa 66:2, New International Version

King David, himself perhaps the most qualified of all men to speak on the matter of the heart, echoes the simple and profound truth of God in his anguished lamenting found in Psalm 51:

For You do not delight in sacrifice, otherwise I would give it;

> You are not pleased with burnt offering.
> The sacrifices of God are a broken spirit;
> A broken and a contrite heart, O God, You will not despise.[56]

Above all else this is the simple articulation of what God wants: a broken, contrite, and humble heart. Here is the heart of God, the perfect truth of His expressed desire. In many ways this insight into the desire and mind of God represents the "keys to the kingdom" as it were.

What an alarming revelation this reality can be for many of us. The simplicity of the imperative makes it seem somehow incomplete. "There must be more," we insist. "Surely God wants this or that from me - stewardship, holiness, perhaps charity" - in addition to humility and contrition. And surely He wants more FOR me - "life, prosperity, success, joy" - than He wants for me a broken heart. And yet here is the truth nonetheless, and we all the more as leaders must confront the truth of scripture. Humility and contrition are what God desires above all else from me. A broken heart is what He desires for me.

Certainly this is not the stuff of Sunday School. God's desire for brokenness and contrition from His children is a truth that seems strangely at odds with some of today's popular imaginings of God. Some of today's user friendly conceptions of God have spawned the pseudo-evangelistic phrases such as: "God loves you and has a wonderful plan for your life," or "Give your heart to

---

[56] Ps 51:17

Jesus." How would such phrases be transformed by this truth of God's word? "Give your heart to Jesus so that He might rightly break it?" Perhaps.

If we need to bolster our confidence in the plain truth of this scripture we may consider all of the teachings and words of Christ: the last shall be first[57], the contrition of Zacchaeus[58], the Sermon on the Mount (blessed are the poor in spirit)[59], Christ's self-description, "I am gentle and humble in heart"[60], Isaiah 61 - "He has sent me (Christ) to bind up the brokenhearted"[61], and the humiliation of Christ in His suffering, are only a few examples.

In 1692 the great theologian John Bunyan published The Acceptable Sacrifice, a book that stands to this day as perhaps the greatest Christian work regarding the character and condition of heart which is pleasing to God. In both of our lives this particular work of Bunyan's has produced enormous growth and challenge. We would highly recommend The Acceptable Sacrifice to any believer, and in particular we strongly commend the reading of it to any Christian business leader. It is available at many Christian bookstore (although they may need to order it for you), but more conveniently the text of the book (and all of Bunyan's works) are available for free download at several internet sites. A simple search for: << "John Bunyan" "Acceptable Sacrifice" "download" >> will produce several options.

We are deliberate here to mention Bunyan's landmark work because it is from it that we have developed much of the material which follows regarding to the fruit of a broken and contrite heart.

No doubt we see now only through a glass darkly, but one of the wonderful mysteries of our God is that He is without contradiction. All of the truths

---

[57] Matt 20:16
[58] Luke 19:8
[59] Matt 5:3
[60] Matt 11:29
[61] Isa 61:1

of God are reconcilable and perfect. In combination the three realizations: 1.) that the heart is all that matters to God, 2.) that the natural condition of our hearts is wicked, and 3.) That the desire God has for our hearts is that they be humble, contrite and broken - are for many of us not immediately reconcilable with our knowledge of a loving God. Our faith is rooted in the firm foundation of His person - His sacrificial love, extravagant grace, abounding mercy, ceaseless creativity, infinite power, unspeakable holiness, and surpassing majesty. How do we reconcile these exceedingly lovely attributes with His desire that our hearts be broken?

As Christian leaders we must pursue this reconciliation of ideas. We cannot dismiss God's call to authentic brokenness and humility simply because it will not play within the established walls of our companies. We cannot persist in a shallow theology which instructs a leadership style that is comfortably fashioned after the world, and only brightly decorated with a sparkling ring of religion. God desires and demands more from His leaders. At various times recorded in the Bible He has had His leaders running for their lives, hiding in caves, wandering for years, murdered, weeping on the floor, and marching into war. His unchangeable nature assures us that His desire for the hearts of those leaders are the same desires He has for ours. It is our fervent belief that these 'heart' truths, and a right understanding of them, do indeed contain within them the 'keys to the kingdom'.

So, instructed by Bunyan, let's consider the nature of the heart that is broken and contrite.

Contrition vs. Attrition

Contrition is a fairly infrequently used word. When President Clinton was facing investigation and impeachment, there was wide speculation over the degree to which he was contrite. This use seemed to imply an authentic and heart-felt sorrow. When considering whether the President was contrite, the pundits seemed to be asking, "Is he truly sorry?" This use captures half of the original definition of contrition but misses the word's most important distinction.

Contrition is: *a deep sorrow over sin which results from a direct understanding of the sin's offense to God.* The motivation for the sorrow of the contrite person originates solely from that individual's relationship with God. They weep because they have grieved God. Certainly the network and newspaper pundits did not intend to speculate on the President's relationship with God.

Considering what a word does not mean often can help to better understand that word. The opposite of contrition is attrition. If God loves and desires a contrite heart, then surely He hates its opposite. Attrition is: *a deep sorrow over sin which results from a direct understanding of the punishment and consequences of that sin.* The motivation for the sorrow of the attrite person originates from the individual's relationship to themselves. The layman's expression is, "I'm sorry I got caught." They consider the consequences of their sin and, weighing the cost of punishment, they are filled with sorrow at what they have lost. Perhaps attrition would have been a better word for the pundits as they considered the heart of the President.

In the story of King David and Bathsheba we are given perfect illustrations of both attrition and contrition. It is the story which is behind Psalm 51, the psalm in which David declares, "The sacrifices of God are a broken spirit; A broken and a contrite heart, O God, You will not despise." In the heart wrenching Psalm, the King is lamenting a horrible sin of his own heart.

Having coveted Bathsheba, the wife of one of his own loyal soldiers who is away fighting in his army, David seduces and sleeps with her. When David learns that Bathsheba has conceived his child the King fears his adulterous sin will be discovered. So he summons Bathsheba's husband, Uriah, home from the battle so that Uriah will sleep with his wife and the sin will be covered up. But the honor and duty of Uriah leads the soldier to refuse the comforts of his home and the embrace of his wife so long as the battle rages on without him. Desperate, King David returns his faithful soldier to the fight with a note for Uriah's commanding officer; a note which Uriah does not read but dutifully delivers to his commander. It reads, "Set Uriah in the forefront of the hottest battle, and retreat from him, that he may be struck down and die."[62] The King's wicked plan is completed and Uriah is killed.

Here we have the man known before all other men as the 'man after God's own heart'; an adulterer, deceiver, and murderer. This is a man who had his own good soldier killed so that he might avoid shame, a King foolishly striving to cover sin with sin. And yet this is also the one through whom the royal line of the messiah, the King of Kings, would be established. How are we to understand God's affection for David? If the heart is indeed the seat of desire, seat of will, and seat of passion are not David's crimes, crimes of the heart? And yet how can the heart of David, a heart that led him to the height of wickedness, be the same heart that God says is after His very own?

The Leader Exposed

Far from contrite, we see first the attrition of David. Bathsheba's pregnancy threatens to expose David's sin of adultery and it is the King's fear of that exposure that guides his actions. David's sorrow, as it were, is derived from an awareness of the potential consequences of his sin. It is David's attrition, his sense of self-preservation which grows from his relationship to himself, that leads the King deeper into sin.

Yet in Psalm 51, written in the aftermath of David's sin, it is a contrite heart that David experiences and finds pleasing to God. What has David experienced? As the story continues, we see the prophet Nathan delivering to David the truth of God - that David's sin, and his heart, has not escaped the eyes of God. In a moment, David is utterly exposed before his God. The

---

[62] 2 Sam 11:15-16

reality of his wickedness in the face of a Holy God is inescapably before him and a single realization shatters the King. He cries out:

> Against You, You only, I have sinned
> And done what is evil in Your sight[63]

David tears his clothes and languishes upon the floor of his court. Not against Bathsheba nor Uriah has he sinned but against God Almighty himself. In that piercing reality David's previous cares for the opinions and judgments of his kingdom and contemporaries vanishes. The consequences of shame and disgrace which fed his attrition are no longer of any consequence at all. In the face of his transgression against God, all else is dim.

David is experiencing a shattering born out of a radical awareness of the wickedness of his own heart revealed before the holiness of God. In that experience God, in his grace, forged in David a heart that was pleasing to Him: a broken and contrite heart. Not born out of sorrow for the death of Uriah or the seduction of Bathsheba, David's new heart is fashioned solely out of the stark reality of his sin against God.

How is it then that David, an adulterer and murderer, is a man after God's own heart? Because it is the heart that matters to God, it is the heart God sees. Let's return then for a moment to the seeming spiritual conundrum that we left at the chapter's beginning.

Remember that we were brought to the conclusion that to confront the reality of a 'heart-centric' understanding of leadership is to also confront the devastating effects of sin and the certainty of the sickness of the heart. The natural sinful condition of man would seem to dictate that a heart-centric view of leadership would only lead to wicked organizations.

---

[63] Ps 51:4

We wondered then if there is any point to developing an understanding (however correct) of the centrality of a leader's heart within an organization if that heart is assuredly wicked? What good is the light of truth when it reveals depravity?

It is in fact exactly at that point, the point when the full light of God's Holy presence is brought to bear upon the wicked heart, that produces the brokenness and sorrowful contrition that is pleasing to God. How then do we reconcile the exceedingly lovely attributes of God with His simultaneous desire that we be broken and sorrowfully contrite? When we come to an understanding that brokenness and contrition is the only response possible when we do in fact confront the very Person and Presence, the sacrificial love, extravagant grace, abounding mercy, ceaseless creativity, infinite power, unspeakable holiness, and surpassing majesty of the Living God. Simply put, God loves the reality of the human heart that is exposed before Him. The heart that hides from the light of God, that paints a veneer of performance and piety around it cannot be rightly broken or contrite. It is instead the leader's heart that surrenders to God, exposed in the reality of its wickedness, naked and trembling before the Lord that is the heart which will be made rightly broken and contrite after His.

Broken Hearted Leader

In The Acceptable Sacrifice, Bunyan laid out 6 characteristics of a broken and contrite heart, which we have co-opted and called "The 6 fruits of a Broken Hearted Leader".

1. **God esteems and desires a broken and a contrite heart above any other sacrifices a leader can offer.**

In Psalm 51 David says:

> For You do not delight in sacrifice, otherwise I would give it;
> You are not pleased with burnt offering.
> The sacrifices of God are a broken spirit;
> A broken and a contrite heart, O God, You will not despise.[64]

As leaders we so often justify the pursuit of a bigger company, more money, a more efficient organization with the thought that we will offer our success as a sacrifice to God. God is clear that if our hearts are not broken and contrite, then He has no use for our sacrifices of any kind. What, after all, can we offer to the God of the Universe which is not already His?

What a liberating realization: As a leader God simply desires my authentic heart, humbled and broken before him. Above all external possessions and duties, above all deeds and words, more precious than a $1 million donation to the church, more desired than a thriving company bible study, God esteems a leader's broken heart.

2. God values a leader's broken and contrite heart over all of heaven and all of earth.

Consider that statement again. Above all that is upon the earth, above all of creation in all of its splendor, God values a single broken and contrite heart. Above all the riches that are contained upon the earth. Above all the stars and the universes of the heavens, worlds unimagined and unnamed, God values the broken and contrite heart of a business leader. What extravagance! It is a thrilling idea whose promise is almost too much to believe. But there it is in Isaiah 66. First God lays out the totality of His creation and His dominion and His sovereignty over it:

---

[64] Ps 51:16-17

Heaven is My throne and the earth is My footstool.

Where then is a house you could build for Me?

And where is a place that I may rest?

For My hand made all these things,

Thus all these things came into being," declares the LORD.

He reminds us of His perfect sufficiency. "What can you build or do or make for me", he asks? Then the Lord says simply this:

But to this one I will look,

To him who is humble and contrite of spirit, and who trembles at My word.[65]

It is here that the splendor of God's divine paradox begins to develop before us: It is the heart that has realized its absolute unworthiness that is at once of supreme worth to God.

3. **God desires the brokenhearted and contrite leader as a companion.**

I dwell on a high and holy place,

And also with the contrite and lowly of spirit[66]

This is another stunning truth of God. That He chooses to dwell, to live, to walk, to speak with the broken and contrite, and that He chooses no other. It is not the intelligent, the successful, the earnest, or the strong that He chooses to fellowship with, but the broken and the contrite.

As Christian business leaders the presence of God in our lives, and the joys and fruits of fellowship with Him, must be more than an abstracted notion. The living and moving presence of God Almighty is an unmistakable reality. If

---

[65] Isa 66:1-2

[66] Isa 57:15

we assume the favor of God's presence in our lives based upon an entitlement which we have cultivated even through Christian practices, we risk the gravest of penalties. The living God is clear about exactly who it is that He chooses to dwell with - and it is only the broken, humble, and contrite. That divine dwelling presence or its absence is the single great divider among leaders in this age and in ages past.

Can the Christian really function upon the current corporate landscape as a brokenhearted leader? The answer is perhaps found in another question. Can the Christian lead without God's presence?

But what a glorious reality for the brokenhearted. The eternal and majestic God, who dwells in the heavens in His entire splendor, also chooses to dwell with that humble leader. Even more, that God's desire for companionship is so complete that He will do the breaking in a business leader so He might have a suitable companion to enjoy the blessing of His fellowship. This is an extraordinary comfort and promise to the Christian business leader as they move into a more wholehearted approach to their work. The necessary shedding of the methods, motivations, securities, and habits of old at first seems to provoke in the leader thoughts of complete annihilation: "I am a hypocrite," "I will lose my job and my leadership," "I will forfeit my plans and designs," "I will lose everything." And yet no sooner are those fears faced than they are erased by the perfect peace that comes with the presence of God. As the lyrics of the classic hymn "Amazing Grace" declare, "Was grace that taught my heart to fear; And grace my fears relieved."

4. God's touch and comfort of God is reserved for the brokenhearted and contrite.

The brokenhearted and contrite leader is in desperate need of comfort. King David was a wreck, languishing in moans and groans upon the palace floor. There was no one in his court nor anyone in his kingdom who could comfort him. Nothing can help the brokenhearted and contrite leader but the life giving, reviving touch of God. In Psalm 51, David cries out,

> Create in me a clean heart, O God,
> And renew a steadfast spirit within me.[67]

That renewing and regenerating power of God is a power that He reserves only for the brokenhearted and the contrite. It is a power that no other type of heart may experience, and in the experience of that power is the intimacy of God. The leader who has experienced the restoring touch of God knows and is known by God. That intimate knowledge of God and the awareness of His power rooted in the reality of the leader's life produce an emboldened leader. The brokenhearted and contrite leader, restored by the living God, is a leader who fears no man or circumstance. Such a leader enjoys fellowship with the Creator, knows His character, and is convinced of His absolute power.

How much does the leader, having experienced the power and grace of God, and enjoying the fellowship of the Creator of the Universe, walk in a spirit of confidence, boldness, and liberty? Nothing frightens this leader who has been broken and restored by God. There is nothing they fear losing and nothing they fear gaining for Christ. For this leader the promises of God have leapt to life. They are emboldened and courageous, even audacious in their confidence in Christ.

5. Jesus Christ's main mission is to care for the brokenhearted and contrite.

Near the beginning of Christ's ministry, He walked into the synagogue and read aloud from Isaiah 61, which includes these words, "He has sent me to bind up the brokenhearted."[68] When He finished the reading Jesus declared,

---

[68] Isa 61:1

[67] Ps 51:10

"Today this Scripture has been fulfilled in your hearing."[69] Jesus Christ came for His own, and His own are the brokenhearted. The brokenhearted business leader is the target of Christ's rescue mission.

There is tremendous peace that comes with being the object of mercy. Recently we were imagining the plight of American civilians on foreign soil who, when war threatens to erupt around them, take refuge in US embassies. Consider the hope and relief that comes to those Americans as they learn that the US Marines are one their way by helicopter. In a country in turmoil, and in the midst of so many lives in peril, the Americans know that the Marines are coming specifically to rescue them.

Through the trial and whirlwind that is the modern corporate landscape, the brokenhearted leader can rest in the knowledge that they are the object of the greatest rescue mission ever conceived. In the face of enormous pressure, that leader can say as in the song, "My deliverer is coming. My deliverer is standing by."

6. God promises to save the brokenhearted and contrite leader.

Finally, and above all else in importance, is the destiny of each of us as leaders.

> The LORD is near to those who have a broken heart,
> And saves such as have a contrite spirit.[70]

The brokenhearted, humble and contrite is the one God looks to, the one He values above all heaven and earth, the one He dwells with and is near to, the one He comforts, the one He came to rescue, and finally the one that He saves.

---

[69] Luke 4:21

[70] Ps 34:18

Perhaps the most used up and spent of the Christian-ese words, what does 'saved' mean? Salvation is the very aim of the Gospel, to the glory of Jesus Christ, and we should do our very best to recapture the authentic meaning and significance of the word. Here is how Bunyan puts the saving of the brokenhearted and contrite,

> "To save, is to forgive; for without forgiveness of sins we cannot
> be saved. To save, is to preserve one in this miserable world, and
> to deliver one from all those devils, temptations, snares, and
> destructions that would, were we not kept, were we not preserved
> of God, destroy us body and soul for ever. To save, is to bring a
> man body and soul to glory, and to give him an eternal mansion
> house in heaven, that he may dwell in the presence of this good
> God, and the Lord Jesus, and to sing to them the songs of his
> redemption for ever and ever. This it is to be saved; nor can any
> thing less than this complete the salvation of the sinner. Now, this
> is to be the lot of him that is of a broken heart, and the end that
> God will make with him that is of a contrite spirit. 'He saveth such
> as be contrite of spirit.' He saveth such! This is excellent!"[71]

A Paradox Reconciled

For each of us as leaders, consideration of this heart-centric view of leadership began problematically. Seemingly irreconcilable principles are presented and the vision for wholehearted leadership appears too drastic and dramatic to survive in the reality of today's business world. Even the term, 'brokenhearted leader' presents us with an apparent oxymoron.

And yet scripture clearly reveals to us that the brokenhearted, humble, and contrite heart is the only heart that God desires. Moreover, that the extravagant riches of Christ - eternal life, fellowship with the Father, peace,

---

[71] "The Acceptable Sacrifice", John Bunyan

glory, power, and wisdom are all available to the one with such a heart. As challenging and seemingly contradictory as it may have seemed, the position of the brokenhearted leader in God's economy demands that we not only consider such a heart, but that we pursue it. Brokenness, contrition, and humility have become more than just excellent suggestions for the character of Christian leaders. They are the absolute imperative of authentic Christian leadership.

At the beginning of the chapter we considered the heart-centric approach to business: that the heart of the leader determines nearly everything about the direction, methods, impact, and success of the organization that they lead. Then we considered the heart and confronted its wickedness, "The heart is more deceitful than all else and is desperately sick"[72] Those simple truths led us to ask the questions: Is there any point to developing an understanding (however correct) of the centrality of a leader's heart within an organization if that heart is assuredly wicked? What good is the light of truth when it reveals depravity?

Now that we have explored the absolute and perfect riches found in the broken, humble and contrite heart, we can at last answer those questions. The refined desire of every Christian business leader is the presence, comfort, peace, and riches of salvation. That gift of life itself is reserved for only the brokenhearted and contrite leader. And the doorway to brokenness, humility, and contrition is found only through the personal realization of that sickness of heart in the face of the holiness of God.

---

[72] Jer 17:9

> *I will give them an undivided heart and put a new spirit in*
> *them; I will remove from them their heart of stone and give*
> *them a heart of flesh. - Ezek 11:19-20 (NIV)*

Contemplation of the broken, humble, and contrite qualities of heart that God esteems should draw each of us to a sobering pause. The archetype of the modern corporate leader bears little resemblance to the leader who is first and foremost brokenhearted and humbled. To consider the leader God esteems is to also consider a new type of leadership within today's business landscape. That new leadership is based upon the pursuit of a purpose that can only be borne out a heart that God esteems, a heart that is after His own. That purpose is a Transcendent Purpose.

We recall our definition of Transcendent Purpose as an objective beyond the individual leadership and outside of the company. It is a purpose which is not self-reflexive either for the individual leader or for the company. A transcendent purpose is always outwardly focused, must require sacrifice, and is intrinsically honorable. For the Christian business leader, the transcendent purpose of their company is a specific corollary to the purpose of their life: To glorify the Lord Jesus Christ.

Indeed to consider as truth the radically unconventional qualities of heart which God desires should not however provoke a wholesale disregard for all other established management theories, methodologies, and books. Remember it is not a question of method, but of motive. Instead, an understanding of the heart that God esteems provides us with a new and reliable perspective, authenticity, from which to evaluate and test any leadership and management methodologies.

Remember that the rightly broken, humble, and contrite heart has arrived at its condition because it has been stripped of all pretense. It does not strive to, nor is it able to hide anything before God. The typical leader's heart is first exposed as, among other things, ambitious, insecure, greedy, malicious, and prideful. The realization which exposure before God brings is the thing that does the breaking. This is the point of Grace; the moment of God's perfect affection in the absence of any justification for that affection. In the face of our complete unworthiness to live, let alone to lead, the Father declares us not only spared but supernaturally ordained to the leadership of others - based upon the perfection of Christ.

What has in essence occurred is that Jesus Christ, the Great Physician has given us what we so desperately need: a heart transplant.

> I will give them an undivided heart and put a new spirit in them;
> I will remove from them their heart of stone and give them a heart
> of flesh.[73]

This is a tremendous verse for all who have honestly considered the heart. The second half, "I will remove from them their heart of stone and give them a heart of flesh," clearly describes a supernatural replacement, a transplant, of our spiritual hearts. The heart that was desperately deceitful and wicked

---

[73] Ezek 11:19-20, New International Version translation

from our very beginnings is replaced with a heart that God esteems - a heart that is after His.

The first half of the verse, "I will give them an undivided heart and put a new spirit in them," speaks directly to each of us who have struggled with segmenting our lives between personal and professional, the sacred and the secular. It is a frustration that continues to dog many in the Church. We struggle mightily to bring the 'feel' of Sunday with us into our workweeks. That dislocation between the sacred and the secular, between Sunday and Monday, is a source of tremendous frustration and failure for so many. God's promise in Christ is the reunification of what was once separated; the reconciliation of what was once divided; the restoration of an undivided heart. That heart is a living heart (a heart of flesh), and within the leader it provides the way to 'whole hearted' leadership.

It is the 'whole hearted' leader (broken and contrite nonetheless) that can infuse an organization with, and lead that organization in pursuit of, a Transcendent Purpose.

The Mechanics of Transcendent Purpose

In this chapter our aim is to outline as simply as possible the principles of introducing the Transcendent Purpose of your heart into your organization and leading that organization in wholehearted pursuit of it. As we will discuss, when your Transcendent Purpose is translated into your organization it takes the form of a Mission.

We have identified 5 essential components to the introduction of a Transcendent Purpose into your organization.

1. Authenticity

First and foremost, the Transcendent Purpose that a leader endeavors to introduce to their organization must authentically flow from that leader's heart. We have already devoted a great deal of the book to this issue but the reality remains a central truth: Transcendent Purpose cannot be faked or counterfeited. All the more, Transcendent Purpose which does not authentically originate in the leader cannot be successfully introduced or incorporated into an organization.

A leader's true highest purpose, authored by that leader's heart, will always be found out by those who are led. The most beautiful sounding of purposes may be crafted and offered to an organization by it leader, but if that purpose is not the purpose of the leader's heart, then it will have all the effect of a $.79 cardboard air freshener hanging in a construction site port-a-potty.

The brokenhearted leader who introduces their organization to an authentic Transcendent Purpose cannot help but whole heartedly pursue that purpose. Their heart will allow nothing else. The leader is the biggest communicator, evangelizer, and inviter into that Transcendent Purpose. The pursuit of purpose by the leader themselves not only illustrates the Transcendent Purpose for the organization, but it also validates the value of its pursuit. By nature a true Transcendent Purpose is pursued with honor, passion, and sacrifice - qualities which are a mark of authenticity. Only the leader who is gripped by a Transcendent Purpose can bear the marks of authentically pursuing it.

The Transcendent Purpose of Brian Buffini's business is, "To impact and improve the lives of people." Because that purpose authentically flows from the whole heart of Brian, his pursuit of it has had tremendous impact on Buffini and Company. In introducing and offering that purpose to his company, over the years Brian has invited others into the pursuit which he has honorably, passionately, and sacrificially pursued. When he asks a new employee to partake in that purpose, he is asking them to eat and drink of a purpose that has already long sustained his own business life. Because the Transcendent Purpose of Buffini and Company is authentically the purpose of Brian, the honor required to pursue the noble purpose is none more than the honor Brian has displayed; the passion that is enflamed is no greater than the original stirring that still resides within Brian; and the sacrifice that may be called for is never fuller than the sacrifice that is continually asked of Brian.

2. Articulation & Distillation

Because a Transcendent Purpose is exactly that - transcendent - it is often difficult to pin down and define. In its initial formulative stirring, the purpose can seem to be not only transcendent but also to "transcend words." Alternatively, transcendent purposes often seem at first blush to be too grand, too sweeping. They are very often wonderfully ambitious, at once impossible and perfectly reasonable. As a result, many Transcendent Purposes are restrained at this point and never introduced by the leader into the organization. The leader has a vague feeling about what they want to pursue but they are unable or unwilling to articulate it.

Unfortunately for the leader, a Transcendent Purpose that is not articulated becomes a recipe for frustration. The leader frustrates themselves because the vagueness of their purpose floats in the back of their mind, like the name of an old acquaintance that can't be recalled, or a dream that can't be remembered. The leader knows it is there and even knows something about it; but exactly what that purpose is they do not know for sure. Additionally that leader will frustrate their organization and their organization will frustrate them. A Transcendent Purpose that can't be articulated can't be communicated. Leaders who have not articulated their purpose may grow frustrated when their organizations seem to be missing the mark. Employees can grow frustrated in turn when they feel that the 'mark' has never been properly pointed out to them or seems to continually on the move.

Joe Niego, a good friend of Brian Buffini and a Buffini and Company speaker is fond of the quote, "People who aim for nothing hit it with amazing accuracy."

The leader who seeks to introduce Transcendent Purpose into their organization must be willing to go through the process of articulating that purpose. That means translating the purpose of your heart into the Purpose or Mission Statement of your organization, group, or company.

Again, the 'transcendent' nature of a Transcendent Purpose poses particular challenges in trying to write it down. The temptation is to write a Mission Statement that is a paragraph, even two paragraphs long. After all, the Transcendent Purpose provides the vision for the organization and, as leaders, we're passionate about the purpose. We don't want to leave anything out. Certainly it might seem unreasonable, even impossible to capture the nobility, scope, and nuance of your transcendent purpose in a single sentence. But we believe that is exactly what you must do. You must distill your thoughts down to a single, refined statement in which every word has been carefully chosen and intentionally placed.

There is a wonderful scene in the movie *A River Runs Through It,* which is based on Norman Maclean's book of the same name. In the scene Norman's father, a Presbyterian minister, is disciplining his son in the art of writing. The old pastor gives his son a topic to write on and the boy takes to the task. When young Norman has written a page he hands the essay to his father who reads it approvingly. "Good," the old minister pronounces, "Now do it again in half as many words." This exercise is repeated several times, much to young Norman's dismay, until the boy has distilled his essay into a single sentence.

Distilling is in essence the concentrating of potency. The less words, the more potent each word. If your Transcendent Purpose is powerfully articulated in 4 sentences, then to reduce it to one sentence should make each word 4 times as powerful. Consider it as a spring, which stores more energy the more it is compacted.

Remember that Transcendent Purpose is a corollary to the ultimate purpose of your life: To glorify the Lord Jesus Christ. The mission of the Georgia lender Home Banc is, "To enrich and fulfill lives by serving each other, our customers and communities...as we support the dream of home ownership." Matt's brother has a financial planning business whose Mission is, "To serve the Lord Jesus Christ by providing compassionate, wise, responsible and humble financial counsel to our clients." Buffini and Company provides perhaps the most concise example: "To impact and improve the lives of people." Period.

3. Proclamation

Your Transcendent Purpose, the Mission of your organization is to become the centerpiece of your entire culture. It is to be the one motivation behind every action, the one aim that every process and every system point towards, the point that every decision is measured against, and the basis that every result is evaluated upon. Your Mission must be proclaimed. It must be repeated over and over and over again. Shout it from the mountaintops until you hear its return like an echo.

The leader who is authentically pursuing the purpose is already leading with their actions. Now they need to say it with their words, "This is what we are all about." Proclaiming it provides context for the actions of the organization's leadership: employees must be given a context from which to understand your honor, passion, and sacrifice. Doing so allows them to emulate your pursuit of the organization's purpose within the context of their own duties and responsibilities. Imagine the wide breadth of ways the works and the life of Christ would have been misunderstood and misinterpreted had He not been also teaching and preaching about and around the things that He did. Many times Christ deliberately says in essence, "I am doing this ...., so that ...." He explains His mission and His purpose over and over again to His followers. His teaching provides the context to understand His actions and the basis for making His Mission their own.

A Transcendent Purpose creates a dynamic which allows a company to make and communicate its decisions in a way that immediately reconciles those decisions with the company's Transcendent Purpose. As an example, Buffini and Company recently began the planning of an ambitious new business segment which increases the scope of clients that can be reached and the depth of material that will be provided to them. In their internal Master Plan they wrote that the initiative will "further our ability to effectively pursue our Mission to impact and improve the lives of people."

When the Mission of your organization is a Transcendent Purpose, everything is about that Transcendent Purpose and every communication is an opportunity to reinforce and proclaim that purpose

4. Participation

Transcendent Purpose is a matter of the heart. As the leader, purpose comes from your heart, and to impact your organization it must make its way into the hearts of your people. Abstracted ideas and pie-in-the-sky notions do not penetrate the heart. The visceral reality of the heart demands that it is only impacted by what is real, by what is experienced, what is felt, and what is known. As a leader you must do more than invite your organization into the pursuit of the Transcendent Purpose, you must allow them to partake of it - literally giving them a portion as you would a favored guest at the dinner table. Your entire organization must be 'invited to the table'.

We do not mean that every member of your organization should participate in the formulation of policy, direction, strategy or other leadership functions. We are promoting neither a populist nor a democratic view of corporate governance. By participation we strictly mean participation in the grand pursuit - a collective, or corporate, commonality of meaning and mission as it pertains to the one big thing that matters. From warehouse clerk to account rep to you, a true Transcendent Purpose should offer equal opportunity for participative buy in.

There are two sides of equal importance to participation: the pursuit and the fruit. Each member of your organization must be encouraged and empowered to partake equally in both.

The fruits of your Transcendent Purpose are the benchmarks of your success as a company. By building a culture around your Transcendent Purpose, by setting that Transcendent Purpose in place of increased profits, you create a culture that values the fruit of your Transcendent Purpose as the paramount evidence of organizational success. The goal is to develop within the organization a shared sense of extravagant and surpassing value attached to the fruit of the Transcendent Purpose. It is such an agreed upon value that will spur your organization to incredible creativity, sacrifice, and passion in pursuit of the fruit.

Because the Transcendent Purpose of Buffini and Company is - To impact and improve the lives of people - the fruit of that pursuit is literally measured in lives impacted and improved. The culture of Buffini and Company is thick with such fruit; stories of lives radically changed, care given, and circumstances improved. Within Buffini and Company, within the hundreds of thousands who have come to their seminars, the thousands who are personally coached, in a community in Africa, there is tremendous fruit. Brian has been deliberate to share that fruit actively within the culture of their company. The story of a client who came to Buffini and Company when her life was in complete disarray, financially strung out and with her family at the breaking point, shares the effect of her encounter with the people and the programs of Buffini and Company. In her own words she shares the radical impact and improvement of her life in a video. Story after story of Buffini and Company employees who have been embraced by the culture and the community, whose lives and families have been deeply and lastingly impacted, are offered up for the tasting. Updates and dispatches from Africa come in and are spread around. In this way, the people of Buffini and Company are actively invited in meetings, in communications, and in personal interaction to share and to celebrate the company's most valued successes. In a real way, that fruit sustains the organization's pursuit of its purpose. The fruit can be shared in meetings, letters, videos, and personal experiences with each employee. In a way, the 'meals' can be planned.

However it is not always as straightforward to enfranchise an entire culture into the pursuit of the purpose. There is the inevitable hurdle that comes with the potential for disconnection of specific organizational tasks from the overall Mission. The stock clerk may see no connection between his labor in the medical device company's warehouse and the company's mission to improve the lives children with chronic asthma. As he works, he may see only boxes, palates, and fork-lifts - his job might seem finite, and he may bring to it an individual purpose (such as his own provision). So long as that employee is disconnected from the Transcendent Purpose (the mission of the company), his job and his labor will remain limited and individual. If however, that employee can be 'invited to the table' to partake in the fruits of the purpose - to see the children who are free to play soccer and tramp through the streams, to hear their stories and to feel the gratitude of their parents, then his job and his labor can be enlivened and brought to significance. To connect the employee and their position to the Transcendent Purpose of your organization is to transform that employee's experience of their labor and their estimation of its value.

Dorsey Alexander Stevens - Missouri - line shoe factory - shoes to the less fortunate

In His 3 years of earthly ministry Christ perfectly invited and incorporated His 12 disciples into His mission and purpose. Living and walking beside Him, they partook extravagantly from the fruit of His ministry. They watched healings, resurrections, transfigurations, revolutionary teachings, and all blessings of God incarnate. Christ also was deliberate to give them a place in the pursuit of His mission. He sent the 12 out in pairs to pursue His purpose. On its face, the task that Christ commissioned the pairs with might have seemed pointless and ordinary. They took no special tools, the had no food, they would be strangers and unknowns, they had no credentials or title. And yet the 6 pairs, having full knowledge of the reality of the mission through the experience of its fruit, set off on a miraculous adventure - emboldened and enlivened by their participation and connection to the grander purposes of God.

The challenge of the leader is to reframe the labor experience of each of their employees so that it 'transcends' their literal tasks and is seen within the grander framework of the organization's mission.

5. Reinforcement

We are, each of us, wayward people, prone to wanderings and distraction. One of the primary purposes of distilling and articulating your Transcendent Purpose into a Mission, is so that neither you nor your people will forget it. But it is not enough to write it down once, to proclaim it once at an all hands meeting and then tuck it into a file. As humans we require constant reinforcement and reminding. It is incumbent upon you as a leader to remind yourself each day what you are all about and what you are pursuing. Then it is doubly incumbent upon you to remind your organization. We are convinced that reinforcement of an organization's Mission and their Core Values or Beliefs cannot be done to excess.

In the Old Testament book of Deuteronomy, there are specific guidelines and admonishments laid out for the character and rule of a king. As today's 'kings' we all do well to consider the direct prescription given in the scripture. The scripture describes the law given for the conduct and purpose of the king, and then it commands that the king should write these things down for himself on a scroll. That scroll,

> "is to be with him, and he is to read it all the days of his life so that he may learn to revere the LORD his God and follow carefully all the words of this law and these decrees and not consider himself better than his brothers and turn from the law to the right or to the left."

The king is to read his Mission (given to him by God) every day so that he does not forget it, and so that he would remain humble among the people that he leads. Consider this scripture in light of the following story from Buffini and Company and its 'king'.

While at work, every employee at Buffini and Company is required to wear a standard employee ID badge around their neck. To reinforce the Mission and Core Values of Buffini and Company, Brian had them printed on the back of each employee ID. In preparation for a large seminar, Brian had a senior employee from the art department in his office. Going over his vision for the seminar materials Brian requested 2 new layouts for the following day. The layouts they had completed had each taken days to develop, and Brian was asking for the near impossible. One of Buffini and Company's 3 Core Values printed on the back of the IDs is "Excellence is our minimum standard." The employee humbly flipped over his ID badge and pointed to the 'Excellence'

Core Value. "I can have the 2 new layouts for you by tomorrow Brian," he replied, "but I can't promise you that they will be excellent."

For Brian the issue was happily settled at once. "How many excellent layouts can we get done," he asked?

"I know I can have one excellent layout done," was the reply.

"Wonderful," smiled Brian, thrilled at the ownership of purpose and principle that his employee had demonstrated.

The culture of Buffini and Company is so effectively infused with the company's Mission and Values that the company's employees, full partakers in the purpose, now help to hold leadership accountable to that Transcendent Purpose. Where once only Brian and his wife, Beverly were set in pursuit of his Transcendent Purpose, Brian now leads an enthusiastic community of hundreds in wholehearted abandon towards a single common purpose.

The Heart of Business   Chapter 10 / **Pursuing Process,**
Relinquishing Result
Hayes/Stevens

And He went a little beyond them, and fell on His face and prayed, saying, "My Father, if it is possible, let this cup pass from Me; yet not as I will, but as You will." - Matthew 26:39-40

How To

It is our prayer that as you reach this 10th and final chapter, you find yourself both challenged and encouraged. We hope that the information in this book has been challenging for you, the reader, in the same way that it has proven challenging for us, the writers. It is our firm belief that the view of leadership which is outlined in this book is not our view of leadership, but that it is the inescapable view of leadership as presented in God's Word. Before we came to the writing of this book, we wrestled deeply and personally with the implications of God's Word as it applies to business leadership today. Indeed, much of this book runs counter to the prevailing way of doing business today. If experiencing this book and, most importantly, if experiencing the plain reality of His Word as discussed in these pages has caused in you a similar wrestling and even a discomfort, then we are glad to have you.

We hope also that as you are challenged, you are simultaneously encouraged. At the beginning of the book we noted the longing and discontent that is latent in the hearts of so many Christian business leaders today. "God has set eternity in the hearts of men,"[74] and the longing for meaning and purpose in our work and leadership roles grows out of the unavoidable awareness of Him which He has placed within our hearts. We hope you are encouraged then in two things. First, that you are not alone in your longing and frustration. If you have carried a haunting certainty that your organization, your labor, and your own leadership could be for Jesus Christ something so much more, then you join a growing community of Christian brothers and sisters who bear that same certainty. Secondly, we hope that you have found the encouragement that comes with encountering the truth of God's Word, no matter how disruptive it may prove.

As we draw to the book's conclusion, the question which may remain is the question of, "How?" We are, as a culture, all about the, "How." The Self-Help and How-To sections in the local bookstores seem to grow and grow and grow. Nearly every business book is in essence a How-To book. Many Christian books are also How-To books. As a people we stand ready to implement, "just tell me what to do and how to do it." This book is unabashedly a business book. It is also, we pray, more unabashedly a Christian book. However, with the exception of a single and central "How" which we will discuss later in this chapter, this is not a How-To book. The focus of this book is not "How". The focus of this book is "Why". In the last chapter we wrote that it is not a question of method, but of motive. In this chapter we will "play out each of the strings" which we have pulled on throughout the book. We will answer the question "Why" and we will see how in its answering we are led to a radical new take on "How".

---

[74] Ecl 3:11

Process vs. Result

As a culture we are extraordinarily result-based, particularly within the business world. To imagine a basis for the justification of an organization other than results is exceedingly difficult. Results can provide the basic unit of measurement for evaluating progress in the direction of our purpose. Externally and internally we measure organizations almost exclusively by their results. Board meetings predominantly evaluate programs and people based upon results realized and intended. Sales meetings evaluate marketing, prospects, and projections based upon results. Wall Street buys and sells according to results realized, expected, and managed. The currency of result is variable: number of clients, number of dollars, number of stores, and even number of lives impacted and improved; but the predominance of results as a basis for evaluation is undeniable.

Because the result-based business approach is so ingrained in each of us, our examination of its implications will be helped by deliberately taking a few steps back. First, what is a result? A result is commonly defined as any consequence or end which arises out of a particular process. A child goes through the process of pulling milk from the refrigerator and sweet cocoa powder from the cupboard. She takes a glass from the shelf and fills that glass with milk. Next, she spoons cocoa into the glass of milk and stirs the combination. The result, likely, is chocolate milk.

In business, X profits can be the result of the total process of business operations for a year. X new customers can be the result of a marketing campaign. X layoffs are seen as the result of Y economic factors in conjunction with Z company decisions. Additionally, results can also be more abstractly credited or assigned to an individual or a department. For instance, we can evaluate a sales person's 'results' - the seeming ends or consequence of their labor. Likewise we can evaluate a department's 'results' - the same ends or consequences of their collective efforts.

As concrete and quantifiable as results can seem, the defining of results is tremendously subjective. Because results are, in essence, marking points, a result can be defined at any point that one chooses to mark. Results are at best snapshots taken throughout a sequence of events. Anything and any point can be viewed as a result.

For instance, say that a 1 mile walk to the top of a hill is the result of a process of 1,760 - 3 foot strides. There are in essence 1,760 'steps' in the process. After taking 1,760 steps we may stop and consider the 'result' which arose out of the process of taking those steps (the traveling of one mile). But, we may also choose to stop after only 1,000 steps and consider the result of those 1000 steps before we continue on. In fact, we can stop and consider the 'result' after each one of the 1,760 steps. This example, simplistic as it is, nonetheless illustrates that any part of a process may be redefined as a result. We see that we can view a simple walk in two ways: As a series of results or a part of a process.

The flip side of the relationship between process and result develops in the light of time's continual march forward. If any point of a process can also be viewed instead as a result, any result can also be viewed as part of a larger process. Even at the end of a mile long walk, there is another step that must ultimately be taken, and the result of 1,760 steps becomes no more than part of a larger process of life.

Where are we going with this? Earlier we admitted that to imagine a basis for an organization's evaluation other than results is exceedingly difficult. Although difficult to imagine, process is the alternative basis for an organization's evaluation. Our aim is simply to demonstrate that there are two fundamentally different ways in which we can view our lives and our businesses: From a result-centric perspective or, from a process-centric perspective. As we will explore, the difference in perspectives and the perspective that your organization's culture is built around, has profound influence on your ability to bring a Transcendent Purpose to your organization.

The Results Illusion

Results-based leadership and management is an extremely popular school of business methodology all unto itself. The refrain, "He gets results" is a high compliment. As we have discussed, results seem to be how our modern business culture is constrained to quantify success. Results are the default mechanism for the marking of progress.

The result-centric school of thought and business seeks as many points of evaluation as possible, providing as many points of accountability as possible. Accountability to results is the bedrock of the result-centric culture. The leader of a result-centric culture often asks employees, "How comfortable are you in guaranteeing that result?" If the employee or the department agrees to the expected result, then the leader and the organization is given license to hold them to that result. Projected results can be managed and even padded, but it is those results which matter. In today's business landscape, results are the very measure of business.

How does the Lord view process and result? His Word again seems to provide us with some insight into the reality of process and result and His view and role in each. The Doctrine of Concurrence deals with two principles, God's sovereignty and man's responsibility, which would seem mutually exclusive, but within the divine mystery are actually at work concurrently. Throughout God's Word His sovereignty over all of time and space, all dimensions, and of existence is declared. He is eternal:

Jesus Christ is the same yesterday and today and forever.[75]

---

[75] Heb 13:8

Jesus said to them, "Truly, truly, I say to you, before Abraham was born, I am."[76]

He is all powerful and providential:

I, the LORD, am the maker of all things,
Stretching out the heavens by Myself
And spreading out the earth all alone[77]

He, "upholds all things by the word of His power."[78]

And He is all knowing:

Are not two sparrows sold for a cent? And yet not one of them will fall to the ground apart from your Father. But the very hairs of your head are all numbered.[79]

The implications of a completely sovereign God have a devastating effect upon our result-centric views of life and business. A right view of God's sovereignty leads to an acknowledgement that God and God alone is in control of all things, from the death of a sparrow to the reporting of profits. A result-centric view of business assumes that we maintain at least some control over results. It is the very backbone of the results based methodology. If not for the assumption that we maintain some control over results it would not be justified to hold an employee, department, or company accountable for those results. The sovereignty of God obliterates the illusion of results. D does not happen because I did A then B then C. D only happens according to the providential will of God.

---

[6] John 8:58-59
[77] Isa 44:24
[78] Heb 1:3
[79] Matt 10:29-31

When we believe that we are able to produce any result through our own will and action, we are attempting to rob God of His sovereignty. If my business is successful it is not because I worked harder, or was braver, or smarter, or kinder, or even a Godlier man than my competition and my neighbor. It is purely because of the will and grace of God. Although hard work, courage, intelligence, and piety may have attended my success, they did not add up to equal it.

Results then are a grand façade, born out of our natural sinful desire to control our world and our own lives. And yet even though we may glimpse the veil of that façade, it is an illusion so convincing that we are prone to return to it again and again. No doubt at the publication of this book we will both be tempted and tested to believe that we somehow wisely arrived at the successful result of publication based upon our own devices. And yet the reality is that our responsibility is solely to the process and the 'result' as it were is wholly and firmly in the camp of God's will.

The surpassing story of God's plan for salvation is a perfect illustration of the reality of process, the illusion of result, and the paradox that lies therein. Salvation itself is a free gift of God by grace and grace alone. Lord willing salvation is the divine result and it is according to the will of God alone that we are saved. I have nothing to do with my own salvation. There is no series of good works which I can do, no amount of money I can give to earn my way into heaven. And yet, in my pride I am prone to the belief that my good nature, good works, or good heart has played some role in my salvation. In my desire for control I almost demand a role in the result. But I have none.

C.S. Lewis put it like this, "No sooner do we believe that God loves us than there is an impulse to believe that He does so, not because He is Love, but because we are intrinsically lovable."

And yet paradoxically we are far from released from a responsibility to the process of working out that salvation.

The Process Reality

Where does such an acknowledgement of God's sovereignty leave us? There is the potential for exasperation. Like the youngster on the Autopia ride who has realized that the course of their car is beyond their control, we may at first be tempted to throw up our hands in frustration. In addition, the evidence of our own experience of free will seems to invalidate an extreme view of God's sovereignty. Most likely none of us rose to positions of leadership by doing nothing. And each of us has a complete certainty that if we were to become 'couch potato' leaders, doing nothing and leaving it all to the sovereignty of God, that we would soon either be out of a job or the leader of a wrecked organization. Furthermore if all results are controlled by God and God alone, what becomes of accountability?

It is no revelation to point out that God's Word, far from encouraging a couch potato mentality or removing accountability from us, paradoxically lays complete responsibility and accountability upon us. Indeed, the Bible could not be clearer that we are 100% accountable for all of our actions and all of our words.

> But I tell you that every careless word that people speak, they shall give an accounting for it in the day of judgment.[80]

The Parable of the Talents teaches us that we are responsible for the resources God has entrusted us with. The very name of that ultimate day, The Day of Judgement, carries with it an implication of accountability.

---

[80] Matt 12:36

How do we reconcile then this Doctrine of Concurrence - the seemingly paradoxical notions of God's perfect sovereignty, and our perfect responsibility in operation simultaneously? It seems that these two sweeping notions cannot be reconciled until we have rightly separated the reality of process from the illusion of result. As we look closer at God's Word, we see that it is actually only the process which the Lord makes us responsible for and never a result. In fact it is the perfect reliability of God that can, in our blindness and pride, cause us to believe that our processes of obedience lead to the results, which in fact are solely brought to fruition by the sovereign hand of God.

Matt has a dear friend whose 1-year old son, like so many kids at that age, learned to blow out candles. The young boy, Cade, is very bright and the connection he made between blowing air out and the extinguishing of the tiny light of a candle fascinated him. As soon as Cade had made that connection between process and result, his dad noticed the next evening that Cade was blowing towards a table lamp.

"Blow again, buddy," his dad encouraged. As Cade blew his dad flipped the switch and, to Cade's delight, the light was extinguished. For several months, so long as someone was near the light switch, the little boy believed that his little puffs of breath were blowing out the lights. The anecdote is plain enough.

In business, our standard operating procedure is like this: We want to achieve this amount of growth, open these new markets, launch this new product, or install this new training program. To arrive at that result we believe we can formulate a series of actions, a process, perhaps the one we have learned through training or by experience. We make a plan, to one degree or another, and we lead our organization through the steps to arrive at the desired result. When the result is achieved it further reinforces our belief in the connection between the processes we followed and the result we arrived at. And yet before the truth and reality of God's sovereignty and scripture, that connection seems to be but an illusion.

The story and life of Moses and his leadership provide many perfect illustrations of this truth. Moses was not responsible for the miraculous acts which God did through him. He was responsible for following the process that God laid out before Moses. God told Moses to go before Pharaoh and throw his staff down on the ground, and it was Moses' responsibility to do so. In God's sovereignty He turned that staff into a snake.

In what seemed like a hopeless situation with an army, which was intent on slaughter, bearing down from the rear, and the Red Sea blocking the way of escape for his people, God told Moses to dip the staff in the water. As ridiculous as it may have seemed at the moment, Moses was responsible for obeying God. The splitting of the sea, saving of the Israelites, and the destruction of Pharaoh's army was in God's hand.

Over and over, Moses as a leader is called by God to a process and forced to leave the results in the hands of God. The seeming disconnection between the processes God gives to Moses and the results that God provides after that process is followed can give us a wonderful new perspective on the reality of the disconnection between our processes and their perceived results. Certainly it was not a magic staff that Moses had, and Moses had no power unto himself. He did not turn the staff to a snake, send plagues upon Egypt, part the Red Sea, or provide Mana to the people. God did. Moses was simply responsible to do the seemingly simple processes that God laid before him. "Say this to Pharaoh, Moses," "Lay down the stick, Moses," "Pick up the stick, Moses," "Dip the stick in the water, Moses". "Hide behind this rock, Moses." All of these are processes that Moses was responsible for.

Perhaps God, in his graciousness, created such a disconnection between the processes he called Moses to and the miracles which followed in order to protect Moses from the illusion that Moses himself was causing the miracles. After all when the process and the 'result' are closely linked we are more apt to take possession of the result. I pray each day for more volunteers in the youth program at my Church and in a month our volunteer team has doubled. "My prayer worked!" I am more than likely to exclaim. We implement a new comprehensive sales training program and sales increase by 20%. The sales increase ensures us that the training program was a success. But for Moses the processes were wildly disconnected from the miracles that followed.

Consider the story of the thirsting Israelites. Wandering in the desert they have grown thirsty and they begin to complain and grow angry with their leader Moses. When Moses goes to God with his troubles, God leads Moses to a particular rock and says to him, "you shall strike the rock, and water will come out of it, that the people may drink."[81]

Hit the rock with your stick? An entire people are on the verge of dying of thirst in the desert and God's process for Moses is to hit a rock with the staff. There is such a disconnection between the process and the result. No one had ever heard of such a thing. To get water you dig a well, or you find a stream, or a lake. Hitting a rock with a stick to get water is similar to enrolling your administrative staff in a stock car racing class so that you can increase your key account sales. And that is the reality of God. We are responsible for obedience to the process and He is sovereign to work all things out for our good and His glory.

And yet the inclination to take ownership of the result is enormously powerful. Consider again Moses. Much later in the wandering of the Israelites they again grow thirsty. Again Moses goes to God and God again sends Moses to the rock but this time with these instructions, "Take the rod; and you and your brother Aaron assemble the congregation and <u>speak</u> to the rock before

---

[81] Ex 17:6

their eyes, that it may yield its water."[82] The process has changed but remains simple, talk to the rock. But somewhere along the way Moses has done what all of us do, and he has taken ownership of the result. He has succumbed to the illusion that his process is the reason for the result. He knows how to bring water from the rock, after all he has done it before. And so he brings the Israelites to the rock and as they stand before it Moses does not speak to the rock, as God had commanded, but hits it with his stick. And then for good measure he hits it again.

> and water came forth abundantly, and the congregation and their beasts drank. But the LORD said to Moses and Aaron, "Because you have not believed Me, to treat Me as holy in the sight of the sons of Israel, therefore you shall not bring this assembly into the land which I have given them."[83]

At first look it may appear that Moses did achieve the desired result, but there is a deeper truth. The illusion of result persists. It was, after all, the desire of God to quench the thirst of His people by bringing water out of the rock. God is sovereign and His plans are not dependent upon the obedience of man, thanks be to God. So we see a perfect illustration of the complete disconnection between our processes and the results of God. It did not matter what Moses did so far as it pertained to the Israelites getting water. God's plans cannot be thwarted and are unaffected by our processes. In a similar way, little Cade does not have to blow in order for his dad to turn out the lights.

But consider the accountability of Moses and his responsibility to the process. Having failed to follow the process, Moses is told by God that He will not see the fruition of the Transcendent Purpose that he has been leading his people in pursuit of for 40 years.

---

[82] Num 20:8
[83] Num 20:11-12

Pursuit of Process

What is the pursuit of process then? It is simply and profoundly: obedience. That is the process that Moses was called to. Obedience. Even in the face of sometimes seemingly impractical commands, obedience was Moses sole responsibility. It is the responsibility of every saint, of every figure in the Bible, of every Christian, and of every leader.

As Christian business leaders, what is our responsibility in the face of God's sovereignty? Complete obedience to the processes of God. Complete obedience, is of course, unattainable this side of glory. If Moses fell prey to the illusion of control, so surely will we, and we do each day. That of course is the beginning of the Gospel of Jesus Christ. In its authentic realization it is also the beginning of a rightly broken heart. In the burning of the façade of results we find a humbling dependence upon the complete providential will of God, and the sacrificial love of Jesus Christ.

It is Jesus Christ who is the only one who perfectly pursued process and relinquished result - the only one who lived a life of total obedience. At the beginning of His ministry, after He was baptized, Christ was led into the desert to be tempted. In many ways that temptation by Satan can be seen as an attempt by the devil to entice Christ to take control of the result from His Father. "You don't have to go through that horrible process," the devil in essence is saying, "I will give the whole earth to you." The devil is saying to our Lord, "the process doesn't matter. It's all about results and you and I can get huge results." But the perfection of Christ is displayed in His utter relinquishment of results to the Father and his wholehearted obedience to the process which was before Him.

In rebuking the devil, Christ continued His commitment to the process that the Father had laid before Him. Perfect obedience was the mark of the Messiah, even unto torture and death. As He prays in the garden of Gethsemane before His arrest, agonizing over the pain that is to come in His physical crucifixion, His separation from the Father, and His becoming sin, Jesus' prayer is, "not as I will, but as You will."[84]

Process-Centric Leadership

The bulk of this chapter has set aside the specifics of business and organizational leadership up to this point. It seems clear that as Christian business leaders we are given and called to a view of our organizations that places dual importance on God's sovereignty over results and our responsibility for process. Our experience within this world, and indeed within space and time, makes the separation of process and result extremely difficult. This side of glory we will never fully be free of the illusion.

We can however, deliberately lead our organizations into a culture of process. That is where a Transcendent Purpose is enlivened, activated, and indeed made even possible. A Transcendent Purpose cannot, by definition be a result. It must and can only be the pursuit of a process. Success then is measured in obedience to that process. Projections and planning are subjected to obedience to that process. Buffini and Company views, lives, and pursues their mission, "To impact and improve the lives of people," as a process, and they measure the success of every employee, program, department, and event in relation to its obedience to that process.

As a leader, when you successfully impart a Transcendent Purpose to your organization, that purpose becomes the center around which the entire culture is built or transformed. Communications, first deliberately and then naturally, move from result based to process based. Goals also begin to move from result based to process based.

It takes deliberation at first. Instead of having a goal of "Increasing repeat sales by 50%", the leader may transform that goal into, "Increasing outbound sales

---

[84] Matt 26:39-40

calls by 100%; Increasing client thank you cards by 50%; and Implementing a Client Satisfaction Follow-Up program with every sale." That goal is then clearly tied to the pursuit of the Transcendent Purpose. The leader does this in acknowledgement of the sovereignty of God in regards to the 'results' of their business. The organization may then commit to the process wholeheartedly, be held accountable to that process, and celebrate the results - whatever they may be.

Finally, we again want to make clear that we do not eschew the realization of profits, even enormous profits. Rather, we believe that the Bible is clear that results are in the camp of God and processes are our responsibility. Where profits are results, we are simply saying that those profits are outside of your control. There are many principles of God and examples of His blessing which demonstrates that He often prospers those who are obedient to Him. There are, however, examples to the contrary. Job was an exceedingly obedient man. What is clear is that under the eyes of God, we are responsible for the process and we must trust God with the result.

The presence of a true Transcendent Purpose in an organization, and of an organization pursuing that Purpose, naturally produces the development of a process-centric culture. So long as the Transcendent Purpose is continually returned to the heart of the business and utilized to provide the justification for the entire organization, piece by piece the planning, communication, goals, sales, and marketing will become process centric.

Both of us have, like so many, been blessed year after year by the classic daily devotional My Utmost for His Highest. Each year we have read it over and over. And each year we have found new rich insight in its pages. As we were writing this book the devotional for July 28th struck us anew. He seemed to write directly from the heart of what we were in the process of writing. We have included that July 28th entry here.

July 28th.

AFTER OBEDIENCE - WHAT?

And straightway He constrained His disciples to get into the ship, and to go to the other side. . . ." Mark 6:45-52

We are apt to imagine that if Jesus Christ constrains us, and we obey Him, He will lead us to great success. We must never put our dreams of success as God's purpose for us; His purpose may be exactly the opposite. We have an idea that God is leading us to a particular end, a desired goal; He is not. The question of getting to a particular end is a mere incident. What we call the process, God calls the end.

What is my dream of God's purpose? His purpose is that I depend on Him and on His power now. If I can stay in the middle of the turmoil calm and unperplexed, that is the end of the purpose of God. God is not working towards a particular finish; His end is the process - that I see Him walking on the waves, no shore in sight, no success, no goal, just the absolute certainty that it is all right because I see Him walking on the sea. It is the process, not the end, which is glorifying to God.

God's training is for now, not presently. His purpose is for this minute, not for something in the future. We have nothing to do with the afterwards of obedience; we get wrong when we think of the afterwards. What men call training and preparation, God calls the end.

God's end is to enable me to see that He can walk on the chaos of my life just now. If we have a further end in view, we do not pay sufficient attention to the immediate present: if we realize that obedience is the end, then each moment as it comes is precious.

It is our most sincere prayer that this book has been used by God to produce a stirring in your heart and the hearts of many other Christian leaders. No doubt we all share the same struggles, have the same desire to please God in our labor and our leadership, and fall desperately short the same innumerable times. As you finish this book we hope that as our words fade away, His Words will remain and will instruct your leadership and ours.

May His Spirit develop in you a purpose which indeed transcends the façade of results, that glorifies Him, and that is a blessing to those lives over which your have been placed.

About the Authors

Jeff Stevens is the founder of Precision Service, LLC. Jeff's extensive business background includes positions as Director, President, COO, Vice-President, and Division Head of various small, large, private and publicly traded companies. He has in depth experience in strategic development, corporate sales, fund raising, and personnel management. Jeff also serves as an elder at Valley Center Community Church in Valley Center, CA where he and his wife Jill raise their 4 daughters.

Matt Hayes is a Senior Partner in Precision Service, LLC. Matt's business background includes positions as Chairman and CEO of a publicly traded company, as well as various executive positions with both private and public companies. Matt began his career out of college as an inventor, and has been issued several U.S. Patents. Additionally Matt has served on staff and currently is a volunteer with Young Life. Matt and his wife Bretta are expecting their 2nd child. They live in the San Diego area with their son Jack.

The Authors may be contacted for speaking engagements at:

Precision Service, LLC
29115 Valley Center Road
Suite K-105
Valley Center, CA. 92082

Phone: 888-276-3062
Fax: 888-268-0827
info@precision-service.com

Printed in the United States
41608LVS00006B/262-414